Books by Janice Hardy

Foundations of Fiction
Plotting Your Novel: Ideas and Structure
Plotting Your Novel Workbook
Revising Your Novel: First Draft to Finished Draft Series
Book One: Fixing Your Character & Point-of-View Problems
Book Two: Fixing Your Plot & Story Structure Problems
Book Three: Fixing Your Setting & Description Problems

Skill Builders
Understanding Show, Don't Tell (And Really *Getting It)*
Understanding Conflict (And What It Really *Means)*

Novels
The Healing Wars Trilogy:
The Shifter
Blue Fire
Darkfall

As J.T. Hardy
Blood Ties

Understanding Show Don't Tell (And Really *Getting It)*
Copyright © 2016
Janice Hardy

Published by Fiction University Press.
Printed in the United States of America.

ISBN 978-0-9915364-3-6

UNDERSTANDING
Show, Don't Tell
(And *Really* Getting It)

Learn how to find—and fix—told prose in your writing

Janice Hardy

Fiction University's Skill Builders Series

Contents

Welcome to Understanding Show, Don't Tell (And *Really* Getting It)

S*how, don't tell* is one of the most frustrating pieces of writing advice out there. It's ambiguous, it changes depending on who you ask, and most of the time, no one tells you how to put that advice into practice.

This helpful-yet-unhelpful advice drove me crazy as a new writer, but it did send me down the path to where I am today—this book (and my writing site, Fiction University) wouldn't exist if I hadn't been so determined to figure out how this writing stuff worked. I can't tell you how many published novels I analyzed, and how many manuscripts I studied, or how many sentences I tore apart to figure out how they worked.

It took a *lot* of effort, but it was worth it. I discovered that told prose often included the same words, or the same types of words. I created lists of these "red flag words" so I could easily search for them during my revisions. As I edited sentences to eliminate those words, my writing improved. It wasn't long before I instinctively stayed away from those words in a first draft.

To save you all that effort, I've collected what I've learned so you can put my hard-won findings into practice. This is more than just advice on what to do and what not to do—it's a down and dirty examination and analysis of how *show, don't tell* works, so you'll be able to adapt the "rules" to whatever style or genre you're writing.

Once you understand it, you'll never have to worry about it again.

And wouldn't *that* be nice?

What You'll Get From This Book

Understanding Show Don't Tell is an in-depth study and analysis of what *show, don't tell* is, what it means, and how to use it in your writing. It will teach you how to identify told prose in your work, and where told prose is frequently found. It will even explore aspects of writing that aren't technically telling, but are connected to told prose and can make prose *feel* told, such as description and backstory.

By the end of this book, you'll have a solid understanding of *show, don't tell* and the ability to use it to your best advantage.

What *Show, Don't Tell* Really Means

Show, *don't tell* is critical to crafting a strong story, but what exactly does it mean? And more importantly, how do you make sure you're using it correctly in your writing?

Typical answer:

- Writing with strong nouns and verbs to dramatize a scene

- Using the senses to enable the reader to experience what the point-of-view character experiences

- Dramatizing scenes versus explaining them

Is any of that actually helpful?

Probably not, because even when you know what people mean when they say, "show and not tell," it's not always clear what to *do* about it. If you can't identify where the told prose is in your novel, you can't fix it, and you end up making the same mistakes over and over until you want to pull your hair out. Even worse, shown prose isn't always better than told prose, so simply swapping out those weak, told verbs for strong, shown ones might not make the writing any better.

Let's start with a basic example of a common way to tell:

▶ I reached over to pick up the cup.

You're likely thinking, "What's wrong with that? It looks fine to me." For the most part, yes it is fine and writers write sentences like this every day. As told prose goes, it's minor, but it makes an excellent example of why *show, don't tell* trips up so many writers.

Break this sentence down and *really* analyze it. The first part, "I reached over," is a physical and demonstrable action. You can physically reach over. "To pick up" is an explanation of *why* that person reached over. There is no actual picking up of the cup, just the stated intention to do so, and you can't *show* intention. However, you *can* show the observable results *of* intention. Change one tiny word and suddenly this same sentence shows instead of tells.

> ▶ I reached over and picked up the cup.

Both are physical and demonstrable actions. Both can be observed. You can reach over, *and* you can pick up a cup.

What's considered told prose gets even stickier when you look deeper. Since this is in first-person point of view, the character knows exactly why she's reaching over, so her saying "to pick up the cup" is accurate. She knows why she's reaching. Her explaining her motivation for reaching doesn't feel out of place, so even though it tells, it's not something that will jar a reader out of the story or feel awkward—which is why nobody gets all that upset about this type of tell.

Let's take that same sentence and put it in a tight third-person point of view. Say Sally is the point-of-view character and she's watching Jane:

> ▶ Jane reached over to pick up the cup.

Now the point-of-view character is assigning *motive* to the reaching before the cup is even picked up. In this case, "to pick up the cup" is something Sally *would not know* until Jane does it. She's *explaining why* Jane is reaching and there's no guarantee she knows why. It reads more as the author explaining, and explaining is telling. Telling describes the situation, not the action.

But what if this was a third-person-omniscient point of view?

Then it's acceptable for motive to be assigned because an all-knowing narrator would indeed know why everyone was acting.

And let's not forget stories where the characters are all relaying the information after the fact—as in, the events in the story have already happened and the book is retrospective. Then the point-of-view character assigning motive to events she already knows the outcomes of is valid. Telling in such cases is less jarring because it feels natural to that type of storytelling process.

See why *show, don't tell* is such a hassle to figure out?

Let's try another common tell—the adverb.

One trick to test if you're showing or telling is to imagine yourself acting out whatever it is your characters are doing. If you can do what they do, you're showing. If not, you're telling.

▶ "I hate you," I said angrily.

You can stand in the room and say, "I hate you," out loud, but try to act out "angrily." You can't, not really. Angrily is an adverb, which is a word used to modify a verb (the action) and in essence describe or show how an action is performed—it's not action in and of itself. That's the subtle difference in showing versus telling. You can act out behavior that demonstrates "angrily," but there's nothing about the adverb itself that you can physically do. The only way to show it is to do something else.

▶ "I hate you," I yelled, kicking the door closed.

You can yell and you can kick the door closed. Both show anger and anyone watching you would be able to figure out your mood by observing your actions. You can see someone yell and kick a door closed and think, "Wow, she's acting angrily." Though you'd more likely think, "She seems pissed" or something close. We don't typically think in adverbs, which is why they tend to stand out.

Try this one:

▶ I walked slowly across the room.

This is where *show, don't tell* gets trickier, because you can "walk slowly." "Slowly" has a physical connotation in our minds, so even though it's an adverb, it conveys a real action. We can imagine what walking slowly looks like. But look closer—when you "walk slowly across the room," exactly what do you do? Tiptoe? Slink? Take exaggeratedly slow steps? Move at half the speed you normally walk (and what is a "normal" speed anyway)? Even though you can "walk slowly" and be understood by your readers, the *actual* action can be any number of walking styles. What the reader envisions might not be what you as the author intended.

Picture someone walking slowly across a room. What did you imagine? Odds are a verb popped into your head. That verb shows, while "walked slowly" tells.

Telling gets murkier still when you add thoughts and internalization to the mix. A person can sit and think, but what they think and how you write it makes all the difference.

Here's a common way to write a line of internalization:

▶ She sighed, realizing she'd left her phone on her desk.

Sighing you can do, but act out someone realizing. Again, you can't. You're telling readers that the person is realizing she forgot her phone. The line "realizing she'd left her phone on her desk" is explaining the *reason* that she sighed. When you take away the explanation and put in what someone would think in the same situation, you get:

▶ She sighed. *Darn.* Her phone was on her desk, right next to the stupid report she also forgot to grab.

You can sigh, and you can think, "Darn," and you can also think the internalization that comes after. This is a realistic progression of action and thoughts for someone realizing she left her phone at the office.

To make *show, don't tell* even *more* confusing, sometimes it *is* acceptable to write, "I wondered if there was any ice cream in the freezer," or, "I realized how stupid I was being." There *are* times when a little telling is better than a drawn-out show, and readers don't need to see every little action dramatized.

There's no hard and fast rule for determining when telling works and when it's jarring to readers, but it's something you *do* develop an ear for over time. A common rule of thumb: As long as it feels like the character is thinking it, you're usually okay. But as soon as it sounds like the author butting in to explain things, you've probably fallen into telling.

Dramatize the action and make readers feel in the moment, right there with the character as the story unfolds. Use language and details to describe what a person physically and mentally does or feels, and don't explain what they did, thought, or felt.

What Show, Don't Tell *Doesn't* Mean

It's easy to go a little overboard with the showing, however, so be wary about doing *too* much. Showing isn't throwing every adjective you have into a scene so each noun has multiple words describing it. It's not describing in great detail every single step a character takes from the moment she wakes up to the time she falls asleep again that night. It's not relaying every thought that passes through her head.

You get to choose what gets shown and what gets told, so choose wisely.

I've met and spoken with a lot of frustrated writers who struggle with *show, don't tell*. It's advice that gets pounded into our heads on almost every writing site we visit and at every conference we attend, until we fear that any instance of told prose can sink our writing career. But all it really is, is taking what's in your head and putting it onto the page for others to enjoy.

It's letting readers see what's going on—not explaining what happened—using language that fits your story.

Do You Always Have to Show?

One misconception with *show, don't tell* is that you must show all the time. If you're telling, it's bad writing, and showing is the only way to write good fiction. If you want to sell your novel, cut out every last bit of told prose from your book.

Not true.

Show, don't tell is an aspect of writing like any other, and there are times when you'll want to show and times when you'll want to tell. You'll have novels that work better with more telling and those that sing with a lot of showing.

For fun, pick ten random books off the bestseller list and look at the wide variety of prose styles used. Some will be tight first-person points of view; others with be omniscient narrators who know and see all. Every last one of them will have something in them that someone considers telling and bad writing. That someone might even be you.

Show, don't tell is a problem only when it hurts the novel, and a myriad of factors go into creating that novel. Too much shown prose can be just as bad as too much told prose.

Which is why understanding it is so valuable. You can't use it well if you don't know how it works.

The Problems With Telling

Writing styles evolve and change, and reader taste changes with them. A hundred years ago, books were filled with told prose. Books written as recently as a few decades ago can feel dated and stale to today's readers. The more visual we've become as a society, the more shown we expect our books to be.

Depending on who you talk to or what you read, *show, don't tell* can mean different things. What one writer thinks feels told, another has no issues with—as illustrated by my "to pick up" example.

This is why it's so important to understand what telling is, what it sounds like, and how it affects your writing, so you can best judge how to handle it. The thriller writer who uses omniscient point of view with multiple characters has different needs than the first-person point of view young adult writer. The same sentence can feel told in one passage and shown in another.

Because of this, there are two sides to the *show, don't tell* problem:

- Problems writers face

- Problems readers face

Most of this book is dedicated to the problems writers face, so let's start with why telling is a problem for readers.

Problems Readers Face

Readers might say, "Tell me a story," but a great story is more than re-laying facts and details in a logical order. Readers want an immersive experience with enough descriptive details to bring a story to life in their heads.

Telling robs them of that chance. It explains all the reasons why things are as they are, it telegraphs what's going to happen, and it leaves little to the imagination. It's the difference between seeing a movie, and having someone tell you all about the movie, describing it scene by scene.

Half the fun of reading is anticipating what's going to happen next and how the story will unfold. Readers love to wonder about the characters and try to figure out the plot twists and story secrets ahead of time. If it's too easy, or all the answers are told to them, there's really no point in reading.

What a reader considers good writing also varies. Readers of literary fiction might want as many adjectives and word pictures as they can get, enjoying the wordplay and use of language. Readers of thrillers might prefer a little explanation (telling) to keep the pace moving quickly, while romance readers want the focus on the emotions and how everyone feels more than dramatizing the action.

For example:

- ▶ Monique dashed along the riverbank, sending flowers dancing into the air, only to land softly on the gentle waves before sinking below the surface.

- ▶ Monique raced along the river bank, seconds ahead of the killer.

- ▶ Monique ran along the riverbank, Philippe's warm hand in hers, soft as the flowers beneath their feet.

Problems Writers Face

The number-one problem writers face is finding and identifying told prose in their work. It's hard to be objective, and reading your own words as you "tell" your story feels perfectly normal. Writing, "John was angry about getting fired" is exactly what's going on in the story. John is angry about getting fired and you're writing all about his anger and what he does about it. You imagine all the emotions, thoughts, and actions that support John's anger, but often, those details never make it onto the page.

Let's take this sentence and expand it into a typical paragraph that might start a chapter or scene:

▶ John was angry about getting fired. He yelled at his wife, his kids, even the neighbors. None of his friends wanted to talk to him, and it had gotten so bad they pretended not to see him when they ran into him at the grocery store. Naturally, this pissed him off even more, and it was the poor dog that suffered his wrath.

Is this paragraph shown or told?

Some people will say this paragraph is shown, but others will say it's told—and they're both right. What the writer intends this paragraph to do will determine whether or not it feels told.

■ If this paragraph was intended to be a quick summary to get readers up to speed, and the point of the scene built off this summary of John being angry, then this paragraph could smoothly set the scene and readers would read right past it.

■ If this paragraph was meant to show how badly John is treating his family and friends, and this is all the reader gets to understand that, then it probably feels told and explanatory.

■ If this is from a omniscient narrator, it probably feels shown, but if this is John's point of view, it likely feels like a summary of a scene, not an actual scene.

Look at what happens when I dramatize this sentence instead:

▶ John slammed the door behind him. Who did that stuffed shirt think he was anyway? Fire *him*? That cesspool of an office would wither and die without him.

"You're home early," Maria said, coming in from the kitchen.

"Am I interrupting your bon-bon eating or something?"

Her smile faded. "What's wrong?"

"I don't get any damn respect, that's what's wrong."

When you compare the two pieces now, how do you feel about them? Odds are the first feels much more told and summarized, while this feels shown and in the moment. It's obvious John is angry and lashing out, it's clear why, and you're probably much more curious about what will happen next than you were in the first paragraph—maybe even dreading what John might do.

This is why it's hard to spot told prose. Often, told prose stands out when compared to how the rest of the novel is written. A tiny bit of detached, explanatory prose here and there blends in and bothers no one, but use a lot of it, and the entire novel feels flat.

The second major problem writers face is that both readers and others writers have different opinions on:

- How much telling is acceptable

- What telling sounds like

- What to do about told prose in a manuscript

The person who prefers distant third-person narrators will have a higher acceptance for told prose than the first-person fan. The point of view styles are handled differently, and readers react differently as well. It's very subjective.

Don't let this discourage you, however. Understanding this annoying fact is what will allow you to really understand what *show, don't tell* means. You won't be following inflexible rules, but looking at your work and determining where it feels weak and how it could be made stronger.

Why Explanations Feel Told

When people complain about told prose, it's most often prose that feels like an explanation—hence the "told" part. Anytime you stop the story to explain why a character is doing what she's doing, or how something came to be, you're probably telling. People rarely halt their actions to think about the why—they just do it. This is why simply putting the information into an internal thought doesn't work.

Writers frequently add explanations for fear their readers won't understand why the characters are acting or what something means. But more times than not, if you have to explain it flat out, you haven't laid enough groundwork for that reason to be clear. That's an issue with the writing, not the told prose.

For example:

▶ When she couldn't stand it anymore, she slapped him.

▶ Kim ran from the room because she didn't want to see him with another woman.

▶ She screamed in pain as the knife sliced her hand.

All of these explain, but it wouldn't take much to show enough details for readers to understand what's happening.

For example:

▶ *Stop it. Stop it stop it stop it.* She trembled, the words a mantra holding back her fury. "Enough!" she screamed, slapping him.

▶ He stood by the fountain, smiling at the woman who'd replaced her in his life. Kim frowned and turned around. No way was she walking in there.

▶ The knife sliced through her hand and she screamed.

Not only does explaining risk telling, it frequently kills the tension of the scene because you're not leaving anything for readers to figure out on their own. Rare is the person who will watch a sporting event after hearing the final score.

Exposition and Explaining

Storytelling is about dramatizing, while exposition is about explaining, which is why you typically find a lot of it in the beginning of a story. Exposition is necessary to tell a story, but it hangs out with some pretty unsavory characters—infodump and backstory. Unless handled carefully, they can be story killers.

The basic definition of exposition sums up the pitfalls nicely: writing or speech primarily intended to convey information or to explain.

That's also a solid definition for told prose. In writing terms:

- It's when the science fiction protagonist gets into an anti-gravity car and the story stops to explain how it works and what it looks like.

- It's when the romance protagonist has a bad date and the story stops to explain why this guy was particularly rough on her due to her past.

- It's when the young-adult protagonist visits her dad at work and the story stops to explain how unhappy he is in his job and why this is upsetting her.

Notice the key phrase in all of those: the story stops. When the characters stop acting like themselves and your author-ness sneaks in to make sure readers understand some aspect of the scene, you've probably dipped into the telling type of exposition.

This is so easy to do (and so common) that Mike Myers even named a character after it in his Austin Powers movies: Basil Exposition, whose job is to come on screen and explain the relevant plot information in that scene. Need a summary of what the bad guy's been up to? Just ask Basil and he'll explain it all. While this is a clever way to spoof the cliché in the movies, it doesn't work the same for a novel.

However, sometimes you need to explain things to readers so they can understand and enjoy the story, and there's no natural way to write it without spending pages dramatizing something you could just explain in a line or two.

Explaining the story makes readers think you're insulting their intelligence. You don't think they can "get it" unless you explain it, and that can be a little condescending. If you've ever had someone explain a joke to you, you know how annoying that is.

Trust your readers to get it.

Now that we understand the problems with telling, let's move on to why telling happens.

Why Telling Happens

Telling happens when we're trying to convey information to readers and we don't know how to do it within the context of the scene we're writing.

We have all this information and imagery in our heads and it doesn't make it to the page, even when we think it does. We know a character is feeling a certain way, but we have trouble articulating that emotion. We know events unfold in a scene, but the exact details of those events are murky and we're not sure how they play out. We know why characters act as they do and assume our readers will understand the same as we do.

Telling happens when we need writing shorthand. Our muse is on fire and our writing momentum is strong, so stopping that creative flow to flesh out one or two words will slow or stop that momentum. Adverbs are useful placeholder words that identify an emotion or action until we can come back later and flesh out that idea. A single line of dialogue "said angrily" might become a passionate two-page scene between romantic leads during our revision. We tell, knowing we can return to that scene later and develop it into something profound—except sometimes we *forget* to go back and do just that.

Telling also happens when we haven't yet learned the skills to dramatize a scene, or we don't know what details to put into a scene. Our writing skills are still developing and we don't know which of the images in our heads to put on the page and which ones to discard.

Telling might even happen if the subject is too painful to write and we need to keep our distance. We know a scene is vital to the story, but showing it is *hard*. Skimming the surface of the emotions or situation makes it easier to bear.

Telling is part of storytelling. It's going to happen, and it's going to end up in our stories. Some of it will serve those stories and some of it will hurt them. It's our job as writers to figure out the difference.

Things That Affect Telling

Telling is a sliding scale that's affected not only by genre, but on narrative perspective. A novel with a deep point of view is less forgiving on telling slip ups, while a far, omniscient narrator is more accepting of told prose. This is why one novel can feel told and not be told, while another has less telling but feels more told. The deeper the point of view, the more you need to show.

Determine where you narrator is and you'll be able to judge where that novel's *show, don't tell* line is. The two strongest tools for this are narrative distance and point of view, so let's look at those next.

Narrative Distance

Narrative distance is how far the reader feels from the point-of-view character. It ranges from experiencing what the character experiences (close, such as first person) to watching the character experience it (far, such as third person omniscient). The narrative distance of a story is your yardstick for *show, don't tell*. It can help you determine how detached you can be without falling into told prose.

For example:

Close Narrative Distance: The zombie lunged through the open window. *Oh, crap!* Bob grabbed the shotgun and pulled the trigger.

Far Narrative Distance: As the zombie came through the window, Bob reached for the shotgun. *Oh, crap!* he thought before pulling the trigger.

In the close narrative distance example, you see the action as it unfolds—the zombie lunges through the window. Next, you hear the point-of-view character's thought (his response to the action)—"Oh, crap!" Finally, the point-of-view character processes what's happening and decides to act—he grabs the shotgun and shoots the zombie.

In the far narrative distance example, you see less of what's happening, even though it feels like you saw more. You don't see the zombie lunge through the window; the narrator explains that it came through the window. Bob reaches for the shotgun, but now it feels like more of a passive reaction to the zombie than an active response. "As the zombie did this, Bob did that." You're told his thought (the "he thought" is a giveaway here), and there's a mention that he pulled the trigger. "He thought this before he did that." Again, it's description of action, not actual action, so it feels less immediate. It's the equivalent of, "He said angrily," versus, "He yelled and slammed the door." Both get the information across, but one feels more in the moment and shown.

There's a fine line between a far narrative distance and telling, so let's have some fun and see what this same paragraph looks like as told prose:

▶ As the zombie came through the window, Bob reached for the shotgun so he could blow its head off. He thought, *Oh, crap!* right before he pulled the trigger.

Hear the difference? This sounds like someone describing the scene, not someone *in* the scene. You're told the zombie came through the window, but you don't see the action. You're told Bob reached for shotgun and why, but you never see the shotgun go off. You're told he thinks, "Oh, crap," and that he pulls the trigger, but it's all described in relation to what *else* is going on.

Depending on point-of-view style and personal preference, either narrative distance is acceptable. But if you're writing a tight first-person story and you use a far narrative distance, the risk of it feeling told is high. Since most writers have more trouble distinguishing between a far narrative distance and telling, let's dig deeper.

Here's a typical told paragraph:

> ▶ Bob was around thirty, but he felt older from constantly running from zombies. He left the rundown hotel room he and his wife Sally had been staying in and lofted a pair of worn duffel bags into the back of an old pickup truck. He sighed and stared at what was left of their supplies. *I wish I had a few more boxes of ammunition,* he thought. They were headed to Amarillo, which he knew was overrun with the undead, and he didn't want to be caught unprepared. Sally had begged him take another route since it was so dangerous, but the distress call they'd picked up last week had come from an Amarillo radio station. Bob also knew you didn't ignore other survivors.

This isn't a horrible paragraph, but it's not very compelling to read. It's the explanations that kill it—the flat reasons why things are as they are, the telling of motives. You can see the author butting in and explaining why the characters are having those thoughts and actions.

Look at the phrases that make it feel told:

"Bob was around thirty, but he felt older from constantly running from zombies" tells you why Bob feels older than thirty. You see no details or examples that suggest or show how he feels about his age.

"he and his wife Sally had been staying in" explains why they're at the hotel. On its own it's not bad, but it only adds to the told feel when combined with the other text.

"an old pickup truck" pulls the point of view away and suggests he doesn't own the pickup. Minor to be sure, but what's known and what's not known are key to being in a point-of-view character's head.

"what was left of their supplies" explains they don't have much left.

***"I wish I had a few more boxes of ammunition,* he thought"** tells you what he's thinking. Again, on its own it's a perfectly acceptable way to show a thought, but mixed in with all the other explanations, it adds to the told feeling.

"They were headed to Amarillo, which he knew" is a double whammy. It's telling you where they're going, and that he knows something, which would be obvious if this were written in his point of view.

"didn't want to be caught" tells motives again. It explains what the problem is and how Bob feels about it.

"since it was so dangerous" also tells why Sally feels the way she does, as well as tells readers where they're going is dangerous.

"Bob also knew" tells you again what Bob knows instead of relaying the information in a way he'd think it.

For many of these, the sentences themselves aren't bad and would likely work fine in a story. It's only when the entire paragraph uses the same language that it starts to feel told. When everything becomes an explanation, nothing feels in the character's voice or point of view.

Next, let's take this same paragraph and rewrite it with a far narrative distance (such as, a third-person omniscient):

> ▶ The man was around thirty, but looked older, worn out from the constant running, the constant fear. He left the rundown hotel room and lofted a pair of equally worn duffel bags into the back of an old pickup truck. He sighed, staring at the meager supplies as if he wished he had a few more boxes of ammunition. Amarillo was overrun with the undead, and no place to be caught unprepared. His wife had begged him to take another route, but the distress call they'd picked up last week had come from an Amarillo radio station. Every survivor knew you didn't ignore other survivors. Bob was no exception.

Clearly Bob isn't our narrator here. Someone else is watching this scene unfold and describing it. The word choice, the rhythm, the voice, aren't Bob's but another person's—an omniscient narrator—but the focus is still on Bob. Even though Bob isn't telling the story, it's following his story. The narrator might be distant (and the narrative distance far), but there's judgment in the words used. The voice of the narrator shines through and makes it feel as though a person was behind the words.

Take a closer look at the phrases:

"He was around thirty but looked older." The narrator knows Bob's age but judges him to look older than that.

"Equally worn duffel bags" is something the narrator can see, and equates them to how Bob looks.

"Meager supplies" suggests the narrator doesn't think they have that much left but doesn't come right out and say, "They don't have many supplies left." Meager lets the reader assume how much is there.

"as if" is a judgment call on the narrator's part. The narrator doesn't know how Bob is feeling right then, but is guessing it's this reason based on the previous observation of meager supplies.

"His wife had begged him" tells you he has a wife, but doesn't offer any details about her.

"No place to be caught unprepared" implies the narrator has knowledge Bob doesn't and has an opinion about it. Same with **"every survivor knew."**

"Bob was no exception" is another bit of known personal information like his age.

It still feels as though someone else is watching this scene unfold and telling the story, but the tone changes from a flat, "here it is" description to someone with a tale to tell. It's a matter of voice, judgment, and point of view.

That sense of a person behind the words is what keeps a far narrative distance from feeling told.

Now, let's make Bob the point-of-view character and go for a tighter narrative distance (the common third-person-limited point of view). The focus is on Bob and sharing what he knows, feels, and sees, but the narrator is someone watching *through* him:

> ▶ Bob was around thirty, but felt older, worn out from the constant running, the constant fear. He left the rundown hotel room and lofted a pair of old duffel bags into the back of his

even older pickup truck. He sighed, staring at the meager supplies and wishing he had a few more boxes of ammunition. Amarillo was overrun with the undead, and no place to be caught unprepared. Sally had begged him to take another route, but the distress call they'd picked up last week had come from an Amarillo radio station. Everyone knew you didn't ignore other survivors.

This time, you see out of Bob's eyes, hear his thoughts, but despite how tight the narrative distance is, it's not *him* relaying this information. It's someone else who knows Bob well enough to know how he feels about what's around him and what's important to him. Everything is now filtered through Bob's perspective.

He **"felt older"** is how Bob feels. He doesn't feel thirty.

"old duffel bags" implies Bob knows the age of the bags, versus **"equally worn"** of a more distant narrator who only guesses what they can see.

"his even older pickup truck" implies Bob owns the truck and has had it longer than the bags. Note the use of **"an older truck"** in the omniscient narrator versus **"his older truck"** in Bob's point of view. Bob knows it's **"his"** truck, not **"a"** truck.

"and wishing" shows Bob is indeed wishing for something.

"Sally had begged" is again personal and known information to Bob instead of the distant **"his wife"** of the first example. He refers to her as he normally does, with no need to explain their relationship.

"Everyone knew" is now something Bob knows, not just random information. The narrator is showing all the things Bob knows and how he'd see them, but we're not deep inside his head. There's still a little distance between Bob and the reader.

You can see how minor these word changes affect how the passage sounds. Where you position the narrator affects how detached or close the point-of-view character feels, which determines whether details are seen *through* the character's eyes or seen from *outside* the character. A simple edit from "a truck" to "the truck" or "his truck" alters the point of view and even the voice—*and* changes how told or shown this paragraph feels.

Finally, let's rewrite this with a first-person point of view and see the world completely through Bob's eyes:

> ▶ *I guess thirty's the new eighty.* I sighed and rubbed my knee, hoping we had some ice in the cooler, but no such luck. I left yet another crappy hotel room and lofted my duffel bags into the back of a pickup that probably *was* nearly eighty. It would need parts soon, and we could use a few more boxes of ammo before we hit Amarillo. Reports said it was overrun with undead, and with our luck, we'd sure as spit break down there. Sally begged me to go round south, but that distress call we'd picked up last week had come from an Amarillo radio station. Nobody ignored survivors, not even us.

Same details, but the tone is quite different. The focus is more on how Bob feels and what he's doing than the specific details of the scene. Look at the changes a tighter point of view makes:

"***I guess thirty's the new eighty.***" Bob's age and weariness is *hinted* at now, suggesting being thirty feels more like being eighty. It's an internal thought instead of narrative or exposition.

"**I sighed and rubbed my knee, hoping we had some ice in the cooler, but no such luck.**" Another detail that suggests how he feels by what he does.

"**I left yet another crappy hotel room and lofted my duffel bags into the back of a pickup that probably *was* nearly eighty.**" Instead of comparing the bags to his age, Bob compares himself to the truck. He's had the bags forever, so he doesn't even think about them, but the truck is something on his mind, since the possibility of it breaking down is a problem on his mind at this moment.

"**It would need parts soon, and we could use a few more boxes of ammo before we hit Amarillo.**" Bob is showing they have "meager supplies" by thinking about what they need and don't have. He even hints supplies are running low when he mentions no ice left in the cooler.

"**Reports said it was overrun with undead, and with our luck, we'd sure as spit break down there.**" This gets the information across, but in a way that relates to Bob and what he's currently concerned about.

"**Sally begged me to go round south**" shows Sally's difference of opinion on what to do, and again, it doesn't explain their relationship. She's just there.

"**but that distress call we'd picked up last week had come from an Amarillo radio station.**" Here's the reason they're going to Amarillo, and why he's not heeding Sally's advice.

"**Nobody ignored survivors, not even us.**" His thoughts on doing what's right—with the subtle suggestion that maybe they don't always play by the rules.

Same details, but the tight point of view puts it all in Bob's perspective and everything is colored by what he knows and how he feels.

So much of showing is letting readers observe the scene through action, dialogue, or internalization, and letting them figure out the whys from those observations. No matter where your narrator is or how distant you keep your reader, you want to choose words that let that reader fill in the blanks.

For example, if it's clear the characters were staying at a hotel (because they just left the room) you don't have to tell readers they were staying there. Putting gear into the truck and thinking about Amarillo suggests that's where they're going, so there's no need to spell it out. Wishing for more ammo because someplace wasn't a place to be caught unprepared implies this is what Bob doesn't want to have happen.

No matter what narrative distance you're using, don't explain what the reader can figure out from the hints in the text.

Pitfalls of Narrative Distance

It's easy to tell instead of show and claim you're "just using a far narrative distance," when you really just don't want to do the work to fix it (be honest!). It's your novel, so do what you want, but if you know deep down you're telling—and you *could* be showing if you put in a little effort—then do your writing a favor and dive on in there. Once you learn what to avoid and get into the habit of showing in your first drafts, it won't be a problem anymore.

When using a far narrative distance (such as an omniscient narrator), make sure the person doing the telling *is* the narrator, not the author poking in to explain things. It's subtle, but it makes a world of difference between a story that feels flat and told, and a story that feels like there's a person showing it to you.

On the flip side, a close narrative distance makes it easy to throw in every single thought a character has, so the story bogs down. It's easy to be just as lazy and think, "I'll show everything and the reader can sort through it all." But all that does is create a strange, too-self-aware narrator who describes everything way too much. Someone noticing everything and showing you how they feel about it is just as annoying as having everything explained to you.

When using a close narrative distance, take advantage of the tight point of view. Show the world and story through that character's eyes and only show what's relevant and important to that character at that time. Even though readers are close in the narrator's head, you don't *have* to show every last thought that enters that head. You can summarize a bit or skip things entirely if the story reads better that way. It's all about balance.

Which Narrative Distance Should You Use?

This is the easy part—whichever you prefer and whichever fits the story you want to write. It all depends on how close you want your readers to be to your narrator and/or point-of-view character, and how much information needs to be conveyed that's unavailable to a single person or small group of characters.

Quick note about narrative distance: Some genres have common point-of-view styles, so if it makes no difference to you, it's not a bad idea to use what readers are familiar with. For example, first person with a tight narrative distance is very common in young adult novels, while dual, close third-person points of view are common in romance novels, and omniscient perspectives with multiple point-of-view characters are common in thrillers. But if you want to use a different style than what's common in a genre, there's no rule against it. Do what you feel works best for your story.

Filtering the Point of View

Filtering is one way writers control the narrative distance. How much of the point-of-view character's experience is filtered can make the prose feel personal or detached. Using a large number of filter words can turn a shown scene into a told scene in no time at all.

Filter words are words that distance readers from the point-of-view character, and you often find them in prose using far narrative distance. These words can make the text feel detached. Filter words also remind readers they're reading, explain things that are obvious, and often lead a writer into telling or crafting passive sentences.

Filter words include: saw, heard, felt, knew, watched, decided, noticed, realized, wondered, thought, looked.

The more filter words used, the higher the likelihood of the prose sounding told.

Readers experience your novel through the eyes of your narrator. Sometimes this narrative filter is invisible and readers don't perceive any distance between them and the point-of-view character, such as with a first-person point of view. Other times the filters are obvious and readers feel the space between them and the characters, such as with an omniscient narrator.

A point-of-view character by definition is relaying everything she sees, hears, feels, touches, smells, thinks—she's already filtering for you; it's just a matter of how obvious that filter is. If a tree is described, readers know she saw a tree. Saying, "She looked at the tree" and then describing it is redundant at best, clunky and telling at worst.

Let's look at some examples:

▶ Bob could see three zombies shambling toward him.

▶ Sally knew she had to get out of there.

▶ I could feel the hard metal of the knife against my back.

▶ Jane heard a scream from the hotel bathroom.

Each of these examples has a filter word in it, explaining what should be obvious by the rest of the text. If Bob mentions shambling zombies, clearly he saw (or heard) them. Odds are some other details in the scene will have suggested that Sally had to leave. Describing the knife as hard against your back can only be done if you can feel it. The one filter word that lives in a gray area here is the word "heard." Unlike the others, "heard" doesn't jump out and feel redundant, though it's still filtering the sound of the scream through Jane's ears.

Look at these same sentences without those filter words:

▶ Three zombies shambled toward Bob.

▶ Sally had to get out of there. Or better: She had to get out of there. (Using the pronoun makes it more personal, and more like an internal thought)

▶ Hard metal pressed against my back.

▶ A scream echoed from the hotel bathroom.

Nothing is lost, and now these sentences feel more active and in the moment. They have a sense of immediacy that eliminates that told feeling.

Some filter words are borderline tells that depend heavily on use, such as the wondered, realized, decided, noticed, type.

▶ Bob realized he'd have to make a run for it.

▶ Jane wondered if they'd make it out of there alive.

▶ Sally decided they'd just have to jump and see what happened.

▶ I noticed the car was missing.

These summarize the thinking and decision-making processes. You don't get to see Bob realize running is his only option; you're told he does. The author tells you what Jane is wondering; you don't get to see her wonder in her own voice with her own concerns. Sally's decision reads more like an afterthought than someone making a hard choice. If you suddenly noticed your car was missing, your reaction is probably going to be stronger than realizing you "noticed something." The importance in this example is on the noticing, *not* the missing car.

Eliminate the filter words and you get:

- ▶ He'd have to make a run for it.

- ▶ Would they make it out of there alive?

- ▶ They'd just have to jump and see what happened.

- ▶ Wait—where was her car?

Without the filter words, the focus is on what is thought and decided.

However, sometimes you *want* that filter word if it's important to draw attention to the act (the feeling, hearing, watching, realizing), or it sounds more dramatic with that filter—this works well for chapter or scene enders. You might also want more filters if you're doing a far narrative distance or an omniscient narrator and want to create a detached, observer tone.

For example:

- ▶ Bob watched the perimeter, eyes and ears alert for zombies.

- ▶ Jane closed her eyes and wondered if any of them would survive until dawn.

- ▶ I hoped for the best. Once in a while it worked out, right?

How much filtering you choose depends on which point of view you use and what narrative distance you're pairing it with. An omniscient point of view with multiple point-of-view characters will likely have a lot more filtering as the narration floats from person to person. A tight point of view will typically have fewer filter words as everything is shown through the eyes of the point-of-view character.

Basically, ask yourself: Do you want to show more, or tell more? Then adjust your narrative distance and filter words accordingly.

When Telling is Better Than Showing

Although telling has a terrible reputation in the writing world, it's not a horrible thing. We tell as writers all the time and most of it goes right past readers and doesn't bother anyone. The problems appear when the telling shoves readers aside and makes them feel as though they're watching from a distance and not experiencing the story along with the characters.

Sometimes it's okay to tell.

It's a perfectly valid technique for certain tasks, so you shouldn't be afraid to use it when you need to. If showing is going to detract from events unfolding in the scene, or draw too much attention to what's *not* important, it might be better to tell. It's also better to tell if showing is going to bog down the story or bore the reader, such as relaying every punch or kick thrown in a lengthy fight.

Telling to Catch Characters Up

A great example of an acceptable tell is the "catching up another character" scene. Something has happened to one character, and they reach a point where they have to inform other characters about a scene the reader has already seen dramatized.

Say Bob has just been out scouting and found a huge nest of zombies acting very un-zombielike. Readers have read the scene, and now Bob is back with his group and needs to let them know what he saw. Which would be better: telling a short summary, or showing Bob relaying the scene readers *just* read? Dramatizing it is going to bore your reader, so a quick telling summary works better to keep the story moving.

For example:

▶ "I've never seen anything like it," Bob said, tossing back half his Scotch. He told them about the nest down by the river, the freakish way the zombies had moved, and the almost organized way they'd worked together. His hands were shaking by the end.

"Wow," Jane whispered.

He nodded. "Yeah. Wow."

This doesn't stop the story to relay information readers already know.

Telling for Dramatic Impact

Sometimes it's also better to tell when you want to add narrative distance for dramatic effect, such as pulling away from the point-of-view character to convey that "dum dum dum!" sense of impending doom. This happens most often with the words wondered, hoped, and prayed.

For example:

▶ She watched him ride away and hoped he'd never come back.

▶ He wondered if Lila *had* seen Chuck that night.

▶ They prayed it was the last time.

Telling to Convey Necessary Information

Let's be honest—it's impossible to show everything in a novel, and no one wants to read all those details anyway. But sometimes readers need to know certain information and there's no easy way to do it. Infodumps and backstory are the only way to slip that information into the book.

When you *must* dump, add the information as seamlessly as possible so it doesn't jump out of the story and draw attention to itself. You want readers to enjoy the lecture and feel as though they learned something important, instead of being handed a brochure about the book.

There's already a lot of telling in a novel, even if it's not officially called that. You describe the setting, what someone does, what they say. It's called story*telling* for a reason. The trick is to weave your tells in with your shows so readers never get the sense that the author is butting in to explain something to them.

Don't be afraid to tell when you have to. Just make sure that when you do, you're telling in a way that serves the story and keeps the reader interested.

Next, let's look at how to identify told prose in your writing.

Identifying Told Prose

Show, don't tell is a broad concept, which is why one rule doesn't cover it all. It's subjective, and each telling instance found in your writing must be evaluated in context. Does *this* sentence sound told? Is *this* scene explaining too much? But if you look at only the text, you risk missing told prose in your writing, since a sentence that technically shows *can* feel told. It's important to examine the different levels of telling so you know what to look for.

You'll find told prose at:

- The sentence level

- The paragraph level

- The scene level

Each level requires a slightly different approach to both find *and* fix.

Telling at the Sentence Level

You'll find most told prose at the sentence level. Most of these types of tells can be caught by searching for the red flag words. Keep in mind that "tell" is subjective. A sentence can tell and still read and work fine. It's up to you to decide if the sentence would be stronger with or without the told prose.

Tells That Explain: The most common tells explain the reasons why characters feel or act as they do. They also sneak in when you fear the text isn't clear enough and you have to explain information so readers "get it."

Tells That Summarize: These tells take a shortcut by summarizing instead of dramatizing. They often read as though someone is watching the scene unfold from the sidelines, giving a general overview of the action. They might even sound like a summary you'd find in an outline instead of a novel.

Tells That Convey Information: Many tells exist only to convey information the characters would never think (or have reason) to share, such as world-building details or character backstories. They often sound too self-aware, or read as if the author was jumping into the story with a mini-lecture.

It's helpful to consider what the tell is trying to accomplish when revising it.

Categories of tells include:

Motivational tells: Motivational tells explain the personal motivations of the characters. They're the reasons the characters are acting, either from a personal need, or in reaction to what else is going on in the scene. Explaining motives pushes the narrator away from the point-of-view character's head and describes the action and events from the outside as an observer, not from the inside as a participant. Red flag words include **to, when,** and **because.**

Emotional tells: Emotional tells explain feelings instead of letting observable details suggest the emotion. Often, they explain that a character *has* an emotion, but offer no details or clues that allow readers to feel those emotions as well. They keep the emotions external, preventing any empathy from, or emotional connection with, readers. Red flag words include **in [emotion], with [emotion],** and **felt.**

Mental tells: Mental tells explain that the character is thinking something, but doesn't show the actual thought. These are much more common in medium to far narrative distances and omniscient points of view. For example, a distant narrator might use "she hoped" where a close narrator wouldn't. Context and author intent play a strong role in deciding if these words are causing trouble in your writing. Red flag words include **realized, hoped,** and **wondered.**

Stage direction tells: Stage direction tells explain the order of events as if the narrator knows what happened before it happened. They throw off the natural stimulus/response structure and cause readers to pause to figure out what chronology events happened in before they can continue reading. They can also summarize a decision that readers never get to see the point-of-view character make. Red flag words include **as, by, since, after, when,** and **before.**

Descriptive tells: Descriptive tells explain sense actions (looking, hearing, smelling, feeling), and often signal that something is about to be described. They explain what readers should be able to figure out by observing the characters as they move about the story. Filter words are the primary red flag words here: **saw, watched, heard, smelled, felt, could see, could hear, could feel, could smell, the sound of, seemed, appeared, looked.**

Passive tells: Passive tells are found in passive sentences where the subject of the sentence is being acted upon, not doing the acting. Most often these result from passive "to be" verbs, which create that passive voice and make the sentence feel told. Red flag words include selected "to be" verbs, such as **was [verb]** and **is being [verb],** and **by.**

Let's look at examples of each of these:

▶ **Motivational tell:** Jane darted into the hall because she was afraid Sally might see her.

▶ **Emotional tell:** Her heart filled with sadness.

▶ **Mental tell:** Bob realized he'd never be able to convince Sally to take another route.

▶ **Stage direction tell:** Before Sally could reach the hotel door, six zombies burst out of the woods.

▶ **Descriptive tell:** Jane could see the scratches along the edge of the doorframe.

▶ **Passive tell:** Bob was smacked in the head by Sally as he played with the chopsticks.

In all of these examples, deleting or revising the red flag word will eliminate the telling. For some, the rest of the sentence won't change much, but for others, turning the tell into a show will require reworking the entire sentence, possibly turning it into a paragraph. Showing often takes more words than telling, because you have to provide enough clues for readers to understand the motives and actions of the characters by what they observe in the scene.

For example, let's analyze the motivational tell:

▶ Jane darted into the hall because she was afraid Sally might see her.

The told portion of this sentence is "because she was afraid Sally might see her." If you cut that, the sentence shows. However, if you just write, "Jane darted into the hall," there might not be enough information for readers to understand why Jane darts into the hall. If you've already established that Jane is scared of Sally and tries to avoid her every chance she gets, then no additional text is likely necessary. But if readers don't know that Jane is afraid of Sally and hiding from her, this action will seem strange and even confusing. It needs a clue to suggest why Jane is hiding. Here are some possibilities:

▶ Jane darted into the hall and pressed up against the wall. Had Sally seen her?

▶ Sally's voice echoed ahead. Jane froze. *Yikes, her again.* She darted into the hall and pressed up against the wall.

▶ Jane darted into the hall and pressed up against the wall. *Please don't see me, please don't see me.*

A few more words are needed to get the ideas across, but in these examples, Jane darts and readers can figure out why. If hiding from Sally is critical to the scene, you might flesh this out even more. If it's a quick example of how these two don't like each other, this small snippet could be all you need.

Let's revise the rest of them:

- ▶ **Emotional tell**: Her heart filled with sadness.

- ▶ **Emotional show**: Her chest tightened, holding back her sobs.

- ▶ **Mental tell**: Bob realized he'd never be able to convince Sally to take another route.

- ▶ **Mental show**: No way he'd convince Sally to take another route.

- ▶ **Stage direction tell**: Before Sally could reach the hotel door, six zombies burst out of the woods.

- ▶ **Stage direction show**: Something rustled in the trees and Sally picked up her pace. She licked her lips. Only ten feet from the hotel room. She could make that, right? Branches cracked and six zombies burst from the treeline. She swore. Maybe not.

- ▶ **Descriptive tell**: Jane could see the scratches along the edge of the doorframe.

- ▶ **Descriptive show**: Deep gouges marred the doorframe.

- ▶ **Passive tell**: Bob was smacked in the head by Sally as he played with the chopsticks.

- ▶ **Passive show**: Bob stuck the chopsticks under his lips and barked like a walrus. Sally groaned and smacked him in the head. Now was not the time for his dumb jokes.

It doesn't take much to yank out a red flag word and replace it with something far more interesting. Not only does it eliminate the told prose, it leaves enough mystery for readers to anticipate what might happen next.

Not every instance of told prose is resolved so easily, so let's look at the paragraph-level tells next.

Telling at the Paragraph Level

If the told prose is explaining or summarizing a situation, the telling can affect an entire paragraph or even a page. You'll find these tells most often when you pull away from the point-of-view character and start describing what's going on from afar. These told sections can read like a summary of the scene in your outline. It might even read as if you planned to do more, but never got around to it.

You'll find all the typical red flag words at this level, plus:

Infodump tells: These tells are in the story only to dump information on readers. An infodump often drops in the reasons why something is important in the overall world or setting of the story. The difference between these tells and other red flag word tells is that infodumps focus almost exclusively on information relating to the world. It's information readers "need" to understand that particular story. Red flag words include **because** and **since**.

Backstory tells: These tells explain the history of a character, place, or item and why it's important. Frequently, they're more extensive than an infodump, sometimes using flashbacks and long internal monologues to reveal the often unnecessary history. Backstory tells focus exclusively on the histories of the characters, explaining why characters are the way they are. Red flag words include **remember**, **knew**, and **when**.

The Difference Between Backstory and Infodump

These terms are often used interchangeably, but there are subtle differences. An infodump is most often used to show the world-building aspects of a story—how the social situation came to be, why society acts as it does, why everyone in the office hates the boss. An infodump says, "Things are this way and here's why."

Backstory is most often used to show the history of the individual characters—who they are, how they got that way, the critical events that shaped their lives. Backstory says, "The character is like this because of this situation that happened in her past."

Basically, an infodump explains how the world works, while backstory explains why the character is the way she is.

The difference between a paragraph-level tell and a sentence-level tell is the amount of red flag words and explanation you'll find. When you encounter multiple red flag words and a flat, detached summation of the action, odds are you're looking at a paragraph or more of told prose. Usually it's a single paragraph that describes the situation, but a heavy infodump or backstory passage can span several paragraphs.

Fixing a paragraph of told prose requires a little more work to fix. Each sentence explaining an action could become its own paragraph once it's shown. To fully flesh out the paragraph, you'll often need dialogue and internalization to take it from told to shown.

The upside of a told paragraph is that it's an opportunity to further develop the character, situation, or setting. Your instincts are hinting that the information in that paragraph is worth exploring if you're willing to put in the work.

In essence, a told paragraph is your subconscious writer saying, "Hey, this is a great spot to flesh out."

Let's examine a typical told paragraph:

▶ Bob screamed in pain when the zombie clawed his leg. He struggled to get away, and realized he had seconds to shake loose before the thing got its hooks into him and went straight for his brain. Zombies needed brains to survive or they turned to dust and bones in just under thirty days. He didn't have thirty seconds let alone thirty days.

Do you feel Bob's pain? His struggle? His fear? Probably not, because the action isn't the focus of this paragraph. You don't see the zombie claw Bob; you're told the reason he screams and how he screams. *In pain. When* the zombie clawed his leg (red flag words). "In" and "when" are often found together, one explaining how the other came to be. Even worse, the word "when" puts the cause of the scream after you hear it, so the stimulus comes *after* the response. Bob screams *because* the zombie clawed his leg. The told prose has him screaming before readers learn the reason. Not only are readers pushed away from the action, they have to take a second to figure out the right chronology of the events.

The telling continues as Bob struggles and realizes how dire things are, and then you get the explanation of why the struggle and getting loose are important. The problem with having a zombie on your leg is stated flat out, so there's no mystery to what will happen, stealing any tension from this paragraph. It even wraps up with a bit of infodump on why zombies need to eat brains, which doesn't matter at all to poor Bob, who's struggling for his life.

That has to be one of the most boring zombie attacks ever written, but it ought to be exciting and nail biting. Summarizing the action (the telling) ruins it.

Let's eliminate the red flag words, fix the stimulus/response, and kill the infodump and see what happens:

> ▶ The zombie clawed Bob's leg. He screamed. He struggled, but he had seconds to shake loose before the thing got its hooks into him and went straight for his brain.

This shows, but let's be honest—it's just as boring. Getting rid of the red flag words isn't enough to turn this paragraph from told to shown in a way readers would care about. But here's the thing—as boring as this is, it offers the same exact information as the previous, told paragraph did. That told paragraph only *seemed* like it contained more information because it summarized the action and explained the motives. This is why told prose can feel like things are happening, when they really aren't.

Now let's put some details in there and *show* the action:

> ▶ The zombie tore through his pants, sinking its broken fingernails deep into his calf. Fire and knives raced up his leg and Bob screamed. He kicked at it with his free foot, but it held tight.
>
> "Let go, you sonuva—"
>
> He kept kicking, but each heartbeat brought it—and its infected teeth—closer. Sure, maybe he wasn't using his brain *this instant*, but he wasn't about to let this dragger get it. Or him.

Isn't that more interesting? Same actions, but it now includes details that bring it to life. Readers can see the zombie attack, feel the clawing, see Bob struggle to get away from a horrible death, and see how foolish he feels for getting into this situation in the first place.

One boring paragraph is now an exciting, fun part of an active, shown scene.

Spotting Told Infodumps

Pausing the story to explain a large chunk of information is the definition of infodump, so it's logical that you often find told prose in them. Unfortunately, infodumps are also necessary for many stories. For example, genre fiction with extensive world building (science fiction, fantasy, historical) requires more information to understand a scene and it's common to convey that information through an infodump. Readers need to know how the world works, and you can't always show that in action.

Spotting a told infodump versus shown information requires looking for details that aren't relevant to the scene. Told infodumps shove in information; shown infodumps sneak it in so it reads like the character is using that information to make decisions in that moment—and that's good.

For example, if you're trying to convey that being out on the streets after dark is dangerous, you'd show the character acting nervous about going out after dark, or have him think about it being a bad idea. You'd want to avoid a paragraph-long infodump about the *reason* it's dangerous to be out after dark and why that reason exists. You wouldn't tell readers why it's bad; you'd show what the character thinks and does and let readers figure it out for themselves.

Let's look at an infodump-infused paragraph:

▶ Mardel frowned. Leaving Lord Jull's house was a bad idea, even if getting caught meant his death. Ever since the dark wizard's guild opened that portal to who-knew-where, the streets of Klanduk were crawling with demons who devoured the souls of all they encountered. Those with any

> sense at all stayed in when the sun went down, but he didn't
> have a choice. He slipped out the door and into the night,
> and hoped he'd stay clear of demons.

This explains why being outside is bad, which does little to pique curiosity about what's to come. Since the story stopped so clearly to dump this information on the readers, they can assume Mardel will indeed run into a demon. That takes most of the fun out of it, because they'll be waiting for it to happen instead of wondering what problems he'll face after dark. And because it says demons eat souls, they'll know this won't *actually* happen to Mardel (the stake is too high—death), so the tension vanishes and there's nothing to anticipate. Later in the scene when he runs into a demon, readers will have seen it coming a mile away.

Let's analyze this further:

"Mardel frowned" is solid, shown line, as this is what Mardel does.

"Leaving Lord Jull's house was a bad idea, even if getting caught meant his death" is something that could easily be his internal thought, but it could also feel detached and told if surrounded by other told prose (which it does).

"Ever since the dark wizard's guild opened that portal to who-knew-where, the streets of Klanduk were crawling with demons who devoured the souls of all they encountered" is classic infodumping. Mardel knows this information, so there's no reason to think about it except to tell readers why it's dangerous to go out after dark.

"Those with any sense at all stayed in when the sun went down, but he didn't have a choice" could be Mardel's thoughts, or an explanation. It depends on what the narrative distance is.

"He slipped out the door and into the night, and hoped he'd stay clear of demons" tips a bit into told prose, because he **"hoped he'd stay clear of demons"** feels a little too on-the-nose for a natural internal thought. However, if it were the *only* told line in the paragraph, it would probably slide right by and not stand out. But with the other told bits, it sounds more told than shown.

Since so many lines in this paragraph were borderline tells, let's look at how it reads without that one, infodumped sentence:

> ▶ Mardel frowned. Leaving Lord Jull's house was a bad idea, even if getting caught meant his death. Those with any sense at all stayed in when the sun went down, but he didn't have a choice. He slipped out the door and into the night, and hoped he'd stay clear of demons.

It's a little flat, but perfectly serviceable. But without that told sentence, the rest of these lines don't stand up as well all by their lonesome. It vaguely hints that being out after dark is bad, but doesn't provide enough details to make readers worry at all, or give a sense of what those dangers are. That might make you *think* the told line was working, but in reality, the paragraph doesn't convey much information in either example, nor does it create any interesting story questions to draw readers in.

This time, let's get inside Mardel's head and show this same situation—and his choice to stay or go—through *his* eyes:

> ▶ Mardel frowned. Leaving Lord Jull's house was a bad idea, but he had little choice. He faced certain capture and death if he stayed, but to risk the dark streets alone, without decent weapons? He shuddered. Still, possible death—even soul death—was better than Lord Jull finding him here. He slipped out the door and into the night.

The dilemma Mardel faces is much clearer now, and more interesting. Readers can see he can't stay there or he'll be captured and killed, but going out is equally dangerous. What *might* happen on those streets becomes a tease. Readers will wonder, "Why is being out after dark dangerous? What exactly is a soul death? What's bad about Lord Jull?" Readers don't yet know the details, but they can see it's risky and there's plenty to intrigue them to read on. They can anticipate what might happen without having the mystery explained away in a tell. Plus, with no mention of demons to give it away, when one appears it'll be all the more surprising.

All the information conveyed is relevant to the choice Mardel has to make at that moment, so it feels natural for him to think about it. The infodumped portion flows with the rest of his internalization—thinking about soul death informs readers that this exists, but it leaves enough unsaid that it should make them curious to know more. It doesn't feel like an infodump because it's not explaining the history behind the term and why it matters.

A subtle shift is often all it takes to turn a told paragraph into a shown one. Similar techniques are used when the telling swells to scene-level, so let's move on to those.

Telling at the Scene Level

Telling doesn't stop with summarized paragraphs. It's possible to tell an *entire scene*. These are some of the sneakier types of tells, because writers rarely think to look for told prose at this level. But sometimes, a potentially great scene is summarized and the action is described, not dramatized. It's a scene that contains important information you want to include, but you don't show that scene unfolding.

Backstory is a common area for scene-level tells. In most cases, readers don't need to stop the story to hear the entire history of a character or why a particular situation has a particular effect. Readers rarely need to hear the backstory at all, but it makes its way into the story all the same.

What's really annoying about these tells is that technically, they're *not* traditional tells. They just read as though the author is summarizing or explaining events in the novel while nothing is happening on the page. Readers get bored, skim though them, and complain that nothing happened in the novel. Since these scenes *look* like solid, functioning scenes, the author is left scratching his or her head and wondering what's wrong and why no one wants the book.

As mentioned before, all the previous red flag words can contribute to a told scene, as well as:

- **Backstory tells:** These tells explain the history of a character, place, or item and why it's important.

- **Infodump tells:** These tells drop in information that readers need, but isn't shown in the story any other way. They often describe action or discoveries that happened "off screen."

- **Flashback tells:** These tells use a scene to infodump or explain backstory, but showing the scene stops the story. Flashbacks are particularly tricky because they're often shown, but they're still *telling* readers information.

Spotting Told Backstory

Most backstory telling happens at the paragraph level, but there is one aspect that can stretch into an entire scene—the flashback. Flashback scenes explain why whatever is coming up (or just happened) is important.

If you find yourself adding a flashback so readers will "get" a scene, reconsider. Look instead for details that will suggest how the flashback affected the character and why that matters at this moment in the book. Show how the event in the character's past is affecting the current scene.

For example:

> ▶ Mardel approached the house he hadn't seen in ten years, not since the night Jull tried to kill him and almost succeeded [Imagine the scene goes into a two-page flashback that describes how this event happened.] Never again, he thought. The scar along his thigh burned from where Jull's blade had cut him, barely missing his gut. He must be more desperate than he'd thought to come back here.

Explaining what happened between Mardel and Jull (the tell) steals any sense of mystery from the scene. Readers won't wonder about the scar, or why Mardel hasn't been back in ten years. They won't be anticipating something bad happening. The flashback tells the backstory and explains away every reason they have to keep reading. Even the text leading up to it contains told prose, with, "not since the night Jull tried to kill him."

Backstory and flashbacks are two of the rare places where showing instead of telling *saves* you words.

Look how tight this scene becomes when the flashback and unnecessary backstory are eliminated:

▶ Mardel approached the house he'd avoided for ten years. The scar along his thigh burned and he scowled. He must be more desperate than he'd thought.

Three lines, but it's clear that Mardel doesn't want to be back here, something bad happened that scarred him (literally and probably emotionally), and he's in dire straits if he's resorting to this course of action. Readers will likely be eager to see what happens and learn how he got the scar.

You might ask, "Well, yeah, but if I show the flashback, readers won't *have* to wait. They'll know what happened." And this is true, but the anticipation is what keeps readers reading. If you spill too much information too soon, you lose some of your best hooks and the reasons for readers to turn the page. If the answers are revealed before Mardel goes into the house, anything learned in the house will feel redundant. If the flashback is extensive, readers might just skim through the scene after they find out the answer.

Flashbacks can be useful scenes once a reader is hooked and salivating to know the answers to the story's questions, but you want to wait as long as possible before handing over those answers. Aim for the moment when readers are dying to know what happened and are willing to stop the entire story to find out. Be wary, however—reveal secrets too soon and they might not yet care; wait too long and they might grow impatient and start skimming to get to those answers.

Telling Yourself What to Show

There are some scenes that brush up against *show, don't tell*. There's nothing inherently wrong with them, they're not *really* telling, but they are trying to tell *you* something.

I wrote one of these scenes for my novel, *Darkfall*. My characters were sitting at a table talking about recent events and sharing information. From a technical standpoint, there wasn't anything wrong with this scene. My protagonist, Nya, had a goal for what she needed to do at that table, and there were stakes if she failed. This goal and scene led to another scene that also had Nya talking to someone in another room, gathering more information about things important to the story. It all moved the plot along as information was uncovered and that information set the next plot goal in motion.

But something felt off.

Nya was acting as any good protagonist should, but nothing was *really* going on. All the action and interesting bits were happening to the characters who were uncovering that information *for* her.

I realized I was *telling* myself two scenes I *should* have been showing.

In both cases, a character relayed information to Nya. It was important information, but it all happened off screen to other characters. I was having a character literally "tell" the story to my protagonist. It didn't matter that what he said caused Nya trouble and she had to deal with a mess it made; plot had happened without her. Worse, that plot influenced her decisions on what to do next, and she wasn't even there to see it.

Fixing it took some work, but it was worth it. I revised both scenes so Nya was the one discovering the information in those scenes and cut the "report to me" scenes. And the novel improved.

There's nothing wrong with a summary or an explanation scene if that's what the story calls for, but sometimes you show the wrong scene and there's something mentioned in that summary that has more inherent conflict and is far more compelling than the scene you wrote. It gets missed because it feels like it's part of the plot.

If sections of your novel don't read well or feel slow, look closer and see if you're showing the wrong scenes. Your subconscious might be "telling" you the right scenes for your story.

Common Places to Find Told Prose

Told prose can happen anywhere, but there are some common places it likes to hang out. If you're concerned you're telling too much, or you've received feedback that your novel feels told, start with these areas and look for the red flag words discussed in the previous chapter, "Identifying Told Prose."

Story Setup

A lot of telling happens in the beginning of a story (the exposition), often through infodumps and backstory. Characters are introduced and their histories are explained. The world is introduced and all the interesting bits of history and rules of the society are explained. The plot begins and why the events and situations matter to the characters and to the larger world are explained.

Setting up a story encourages explanation, which is why you find a lot of telling in beginnings.

The common term for this is "throat clearing," and it happens all the time, so don't worry if your early drafts take a while to get started. When a story is brand new, you might not know how it's all going to unfold yet. Or you might have a lot of information you want to share to make sure readers understand what's going on and why all these cool things you're writing about matter. You're in a hurry to tell them all the things you can't wait to write about—and this excitement is good; that's the fun part of writing.

Problem is, once you tell them all that "cool stuff," there's no reason for them to keep reading.

The beginning is a good place to start looking for told prose. The first chapter of the novel, the first time a character is introduced, or the first visit to a location or setting. If you have multiple point-of-view characters, look at the beginning of the first scenes in their point of view as well.

Since infodumps and backstories are the problems in most story setups, let's look more closely at those next.

Infodumps

We talked briefly about infodumps before, but since told prose is so frequently found here, it's worth further discussion. An infodump is a chunk of information "dumped" into the story to explain something. It's like an author footnote, because it stops the story and offers information the author feels readers need to know. Often, that bit of information doesn't flow naturally in the text, it doesn't sound like the point-of-view character saying it, or it feels like information jammed in where it doesn't belong. If you've ever been reading a book and suddenly thought, "Why is the author telling me this now?" you've encountered an infodump.

Infodumps are no fun for readers or writers. As a writer, you worry whether you're telling or showing, if the information fits where you put it, and how to get that critical information to readers without dumping it over their heads. As a reader, you skim the boring parts where nothing happens, and if there are too many of those, you stop reading the book.

Common red flag words for infodumps: when, because, realized, knew, used to, had always, which had been, caused, made, starting to, began to, would have.

Are You Infodumping?

An easy test for infodumps is to check if the information is for the reader's benefit or the character's benefit. If it's for the reader, chances are you're dumping and it contains told prose. If it's for the character's benefit (or detriment), chances are you're showing.

For example:

> **Reader's benefit:** "I'll rig up a small explosive device to blow open the door. That's the way we did it when I was deployed in Afghanistan as a Navy SEAL."

Would the character *really* say this? Probably not.

> **Character's benefit:** "Um, Kevin, where'd you learn to make bombs?"
>
> "The Navy."

This is a much more likely conversation. If more details are required, the character can ask Kevin more questions and draw out the specifics in a natural way that shows.

Luckily, searching for red flag words will catch most infodumps, but they can still slip through. If it reads like notes, it's likely telling.

For example:

▶ Bob walked into the abandoned QuickMart. Maurice used to own it, but he was killed during the first wave of zombie attacks. His daughter Lucille had tried to keep it open to serve the survivors who were fighting back, but with everyone evacuating the cities she finally had to let it go. Which was a shame, because the shelves were as empty as the streets.

By now, that chunk of told prose in the middle probably jumped right out at you. Are you interested in who owned the store and how it was abandoned? No, because you're worried about Bob and whatever problem he has at this moment. The information about Maurice and Lucille is irrelevant to the scene and there's no reason for Bob to be thinking about it. It's just explaining the history of the current setting (infodump telling).

But what if it *was* important for readers to know a little about this history?

Then a few tweaks can turn this from told to shown. Internalization in Bob's voice will convey that same information in a way that feels more natural to the scene:

▶ Bob walked into the abandoned QuickMart and sighed. It just wasn't the same without the guy who used to own it— Maurice? Morris? Who could remember anymore. But his laugh, *that* you remembered. Big ol' Murry behind the counter whooping it up like Santa Claus. Bob smiled as he picked his way through the broken glass. He'd heard through the traders' net that the daughter had taken over for a while, but it looked like she was gone, too. The shelves were as empty as the streets.

Now it sounds like Bob reminiscing about something he misses in the current zombie apocalypse. You also learn another detail about the world with the traders' net comment, so you can sneak in some world building at the same time without readers even noticing.

Infodumps aren't always in large chunks. A single line can feel told, jarring readers right out of the story.

For example:

▶ Jane frowned, because Sally never let her carry the shotgun.

Note the red flag word "because." It explains the reason Jane frowns. If you cut "because" it turns the told reason into shown internalization:

▶ Jane frowned. Sally never let her carry the shotgun.

To show even more:

▶ Jane frowned. Just once she'd like to carry the damn shotgun.

Finding Infodumps

Spotting infodumps can be tricky, but they do have some favorite places to hang out.

Introduction of Characters: It's not uncommon to introduce a character and then provide a paragraph or two that dumps information about that character. Information that provides context for the scene is fine, but if it starts going into history or behaviors that aren't relevant, you might have yourself an infodump—and a backstory infodump at that— doubly troublesome.

Beginnings of Scenes: Infodumps also act like tour guides, explaining what readers are about to read about. They also like to summarize what happened between scenes.

Characters Walking Into a New Place: New locations come with information about that new place. If it conveys information the protagonist either doesn't know, doesn't care about, or would never think about at this moment in time, it's probably an infodump and you're likely telling.

History Lessons: This is probably the most common infodump. Readers encounter a person, place, or item in the story, and you stop to tell them all about them or it and why it's important.

Infodumps in Dialogue

Some conversations contain the dreaded infodump-as-dialogue. Characters have conversations they'd never have, and talk about things they'd never talk about. The entire reason for the conversation is so you can tell readers information. Dialogue makes it feel less like an infodump, because it's characters having a conversation—but it still is one.

The "As you know, Bob" Conversations: Infodump-as-dialogue's biggest offender is a character explaining in detail what both characters already know.

For example:

> ▶ "As you know, Bob, since that day back in January '02, when those aliens came from their hidden star cluster in Omega 4 and dropped those pulse bombs on us and destroyed all the power in the cities, we've been living here underground."

"As you know, Bob" infodumps aren't always *this* obvious. Some of them are very good at hiding in legitimate dialogue.

> ▶ "What if we use the same trick you did for Ms. Klein's math final freshman year? Remember? Where you wrote the answers on a sheet of paper stuck to the bottom of your shoe and held it up for everyone in the room to see?"

At first glance this seems like a perfectly normal bit of dialogue. But look closer. Would the speaker really need to remind the other person what was done in such specific detail? A more natural conversation would probably go like this:

> ▶ "What if we try that trick we used on Ms. Klein?"

Both sides know the history and understand the reference. However, readers don't, so while this doesn't dump any information (and tell), it doesn't convey enough to carry the scene either.

To find the balance, look for ways to convey the information naturally, while at the same time giving readers the important details.

> ▶ "What if we try the trick we used on Ms. Klein?"
>
> She scoffed. "Right, like sticking answers to the bottom of my shoe is going to work twice."

It doesn't get in every detail, but odds are the important aspect of that infodump was what they did, not the specifics surrounding it. In the past, they used this tactic. The fact that it was freshman year to cheat on a math test probably isn't important to the current scene. What matters is sticking one thing to another to hide it or pass along that information.

Catch-Up Dialogue: This happens when one character learns critical information the other characters need to know, and not having her tell the others would feel odd. Readers might even wonder how the other character learned about it. Characters catching each other up on what happened can't always be avoided, and this is one place where a little telling works to keep the scene moving instead of slowing it down.

For example:

> ▶ "You're not going to believe this." I told them what I'd discovered about Kyle's true birth parents. I still couldn't believe they were Chinese spies. "We have to get him out of there, fast."

Conveying information to readers is a critical part of any novel, so you're going to have infodumps scattered throughout the manuscript. Just focus on showing as much as you can and limiting the telling so it's as unobtrusive as possible.

Backstory

A character's past is important to her character arc, but it's an area that can easily turn into a breeding ground for told prose if you're not careful. Too much of it, and it stops the story, kills the pacing, and reads as if you held up a hand and said, "Wait, hang on a sec, let me tell you this one detail about this character before we go on."

While this backstory is told, the story comes to a screeching halt and you risk losing your readers. When it's shown, the information slides by without ever drawing attention to itself.

For example, let's say it's vital that readers know Bob used to work at a carnival as one of those barkers who gets people to play games.

You could tell readers this information:

> ▶ Jane headed for the old carnival grounds. "Maybe we can find the parts in there."
>
> As Bob and Jane walked along the abandoned midway, Bob thought back to when he used to work at a carnival just like this. He'd spent all day trying to get people to spend five dollars on a ring-toss game that only one in a thousand could win.
>
> "I suppose it's worth a try." Even if the odds were against them.

This is a standard backstory tell. The information doesn't flow with the rest of the scene and doesn't add to Bob's character at all. Almost everything is stated outright, so there's no need for readers to try to figure out anything. Notice the red flag words "as" and "when."

Put this same information in Bob's voice, and the backstory is less obvious:

> ▶ Jane headed for the old carnival grounds. "Maybe we'll get lucky and find something to scavenge in there."
>
> Bob sighed. Probably not. He used to work at a carnival just like this once. Spent all day trying to get people to blow five bucks on a ring-toss game that only one in a thousand could

win. Finding replacement parts for the generator in there
was probably closer to one in a million.

"I suppose it's worth a try." Even if they were risking a whole
lot more than five bucks.

Shifting into Bob's head and voice makes this read more like a memory.
It also relates to what's happening in the scene, and even foreshadows
the challenges they're facing. They're taking a risk, and the odds of
them succeeding are pretty slim.

You can revise to show even further, letting readers figure out Bob
worked at a carnival without telling them at all:

> ► Jane headed for the old carnival grounds. "Maybe we'll get
> lucky and find something to scavenge in there."
>
> Bob jumped up on a rock and bowed with a flourish. "Step
> right up and try your luck, little lady. Just five dollars for
> ten rings and your chance to win a grimy old part that could
> save your life!"
>
> Jane laughed. "Have you ever considered life as a profes-
> sional carny?"
>
> "Tried it once. Got fired after six months."
>
> "Ah, how sad. A terrible waste of potential."
>
> "At least I got to live the dream."
>
> She grinned. "How about you and your dream scrounge us
> up a pair of working sparkplugs?"

The same information is conveyed, but it also shows the playfulness
between the characters. It sets up future carnival jokes and a reason for
Bob to be familiar with the carnival ruins without banging readers over
the head with, "Bob used to work at a carnival ring toss booth."

In example one, it's spelled out and there's no sense of wonder or mystery. In example two, it foreshadows and reminds readers of the risks in
a way that feels like Bob worrying about this. In example three, it shows

how Bob and Jane are as a couple, letting readers see (and like) them during a playful moment so they'll worry more when something bad happens in a few pages.

A character's past can be revealed without having to stop the story to explain it. You could craft a quick paragraph or a longer scene, depending on what you want to do with the information.

Descriptions

While an infodump or bit of backstory explains why things are and how they came to be, a bit of description explains what something or someone looks like. It's easy to step back and tell readers everything in a room instead of having the character show it to them.

Technically, description isn't told prose, but it can commonly *feel* told if it's a lifeless list of details that do nothing but summarize the contents of a room or features of a person. You're *telling* readers the details. Often, those details aren't even relevant and the characters in the scene have no reason to notice them, so it makes the passage feel even more detached, and thus told.

For example, try this flat, told descriptive paragraph:

> ▶ The room was small and overstuffed with items from all over the world. Vases from France, statuettes from Italy, wooden shoes from Holland. A bold, green and red flowered wallpaper covered three of the walls, with the fourth wall a solid matching shade of green. On that wall sat a carved trellis with silk flowers entwined through it. Toy birds perched on the top like bright lights.

Bored yet? There's nothing wrong with this paragraph, but it does nothing but state bland facts. So let's show these same details through a point-of-view character's eyes and describe them in his voice:

> ▶ Chuck gaped. *Holy crap, a garage sale threw up in here.* Old vases, cheesy statuettes, those dumb clog shoes with the flowers on them. Bad enough every surface had something awful on it, but did she really need that wallpaper? Maybe she didn't know red and green flowers just screamed "I'm

way too into Christmas and need professional help." And what was with that trellis with the fake vines and cheap plastic birds?

Same details, but now there's a person looking at them so the details don't feel so "just telling you what it looks like." The voice makes it clear this is Chuck having these thoughts from looking at this room. His opinion about what he sees turns flat description into a shown room that readers can see.

You can also convey the same sense of "lots of old junk in the room" with fewer words. Showing doesn't mean you have to fill up space with extraneous details:

▶ Chuck gaped. *Holy crap, a garage sale threw up in here.*

Simple, and it likely conjures the right picture in a reader's mind without the specific details. If the vases and toy birds aren't relevant to the scene, there's no need to add them. You can show just as well in one sentence as you can in one paragraph—as long as you choose the right words.

While a tight point of view makes showing easier (the closer the narrative distance, the more in the head of the character it feels), you can achieve the same sense of a person behind the description even with a far narrative distance or distant third-person point of view.

For example:

▶ The small room overflowed with items claimed from all over the world. Elegantly curved vases from France, buxom statuettes from Italy, quirky wooden shoes from Holland, each purchased in a moment of childish delight. Shelves of such treasures lined three flowered walls of green and red, facing the subdued fourth wall in a solid matching shade of green. That was reserved for the garden, such as it was. Silk flowers cascaded down a carved trellis, peppered with toy feathered birds bright as holiday lights.

Even though no person is mentioned here, the words chosen suggest someone who dearly loves the trinkets in this room. The description shows more than just what's stuck on a shelf.

Examine your descriptions and see which details are telling readers what's there, and which details are showing readers why it's important they see *that* detail.

Internalization

Since a lot of told prose appears in a character's internalization, it's common to have a character think about what she's going to do next, and then show a scene with that happening. The mental debate mirrors the decision-making process that determines the action of the next scene.

In essence, you tell readers what's going to happen next, even though you plan on showing it.

Red flag words to look for: **realized** and **knew**.

▶ He realized he'd have to find a way to get the matches over to the trunk without being seen.

▶ She knew he'd never go for that plan, but she didn't have a better idea.

When you find these words combined with a detached narrative distance, it's a good bet it feels told.

For example:

▶ Bob watched Sally plan their route and realized he'd never convince her to cross town without a good reason, so he had to find one. If Jane was at the office he had to get to her. Maybe they needed something from his building? No, he thought, Sally would never buy that. But if he told her there was a medical supply company on the third floor, she'd have to go check it out.

He cleared his throat. "Um, Sally? There's a medical supply company in my building. It's only a few blocks out of our way, but probably worth it."

On first glance this might look fine. Bob is thinking about a problem with Sally and what he might do about it. But this is mostly a description of what the scene is going to be about right before the scene itself is shown.

Let's analyze it:

> ▶ Bob watched Sally plan their route and realized he'd never convince her to cross town without a good reason, so he had to find one.

This is a summary of what Bob is about to do to resolve his goal of getting to Jane. Notice the "Bob realized" red flag, explaining to readers what Bob has figured out. Next, he states the next step in that goal. Do you see Bob realizing these things? No. What action is *actually* shown here? Bob watching Sally.

> ▶ If Jane was at the office he had to get to her.

This line could be Bob thinking, or it could be the author stating the situation and again summarizing the goal and stakes. The "he had to get to her" is what makes this feel more told, as "get to her" lacks the emotional connection good internalization usually has.

> ▶ Maybe they needed something from his building?

This is a solid line of internalization. It shows him trying to figure out how to convince Sally to cross town and go to his office building.

> ▶ No, he thought, Sally would never buy that.

Same here. He's debating with himself, and this is a more shown way to say, "He knew he'd never convince her..." Readers can see him making that realization. He's deciding his own idea is invalid based on what he knows about Sally. However, the "he thought" tag pulls it away from his point of view and adds some narrative distance that tips it toward the told side.

This is where showing versus telling in internalization can get fuzzy, because there's a fine line between a character thinking and the author summarizing the plan. There are times when you want to state what has to be done to ensure the goal or stakes are clear for the scene, but it's easy to go too far. Trust your instincts and do what feels (and sounds) right to you, as it could go either way in these cases.

▶ But if he told her there was a medical supply company on the third floor, she'd have to go check it out.

This does sound like Bob figuring out his plan, but look at what Bob does next—he says this bit of information in the dialogue, so this line will likely feel told and more like an explanation of what he's *about* to do. It also gives away what's going to happen, so there's nothing to hook readers. The hook might only last a sentence or two, but how Bob is going to trick Sally into helping him is something readers will wonder about.

Let's tweak this and make it more shown:

▶ Bob glanced at Sally, who was tracing their planned route in the opposite direction. If Jane was at the office he could still save her! Maybe they needed something from his building? No, Sally would never buy that. She'd only backtrack for vital supplies. Food, weapons, medicine... he froze. Bandages?

"Um, Sally?" He cleared his throat. "There's a medical supply company in my building. Third floor, no real public signage, so it probably hasn't been raided yet. It's only a few blocks out of our way."

This gets the same information across to readers, but you can see Bob's thought process and how he reaches the conclusions that the first example tells you. It also works as a tiny hook, because you see he's figured something out, but you don't know what his plan is until he speaks and mentions the supply company. Now you know he's trying to get Sally to go there for supplies, but what he *really* wants is to see if Jane is there and save her. You also don't know if Bob is lying or not, because you don't see him state the existence of the supply company as a fact before he speaks. That adds a little tension to this as well. Is there a supply company or is he lying?

If you're unsure if you're showing or telling in your internalization, check to see if it sounds like the character thinking or you explaining so the reader "gets it." The more explanatory it sounds, the more likely it's told, not shown.

Fixing Told Prose

Once you've developed your tell-finding skills, identifying told prose in your writing becomes much easier. And after you find it, you can fix it.

Fixing told prose can happen in one of three ways:

- Revising red flag words to eliminate the tell

- Adjusting the point of view or narrative distance

- Putting necessary told prose in the character's voice

Point of view is one of the strongest tools a writer has in their toolbox, and it's key in fixing told prose. No matter who your narrator is or what distance they are from the narrative, seeing the story through their eyes helps you show and not tell. A simple, stated detail changes when the person seeing it has an opinion about it.

But don't forget—you don't have to show if the told prose is working. Sometimes a tell says exactly what you want for the scene, so evaluate each instance based on what it's doing in that sentence, paragraph, or scene. If a little telling is the best way to write a particular section, tell away.

Turning Told Prose into Shown Prose Without Messing it up

If fixing told prose was easy, it wouldn't frustrate so many writers. While you can fix a lot of told prose with a simple edit or two, much of editing told prose requires stepping back and determining what you want the scene, and the told sections of that scene, to do. To turn told prose into shown prose, you have to understand what you want to show and why.

Hang on to your pens, because we're about to go *deep* into *show, don't tell* and be much pickier than anyone would ever be during a critique or revision. Ripping apart and analyzing a basic told sentence is a great way to see *show, don't tell* in action, and have it finally click for you (if it hasn't already). Let's use my favorite telling example: the motivational tell.

> ▶ Bob reached for the rifle to shoot the zombie.

If we *really* wanted to get crazy, this sentence is full of motivation tells. "For" is an assumption of motive and could be considered a tell. Bob is reaching, but until he *touches* the rifle, the narrator can't truly know why he's reaching. Depending on the narrative distance, "reach for" could be information the narrator doesn't know. "To shoot" also implies motive or intent. Bob could take that rifle and whack the zombie over the head with it, or he could use it to break the window and escape. Telling the motive for both the reaching and the shooting explains everything that's about to happen so readers don't get to *see* it.

Even if we're in Bob's point of view, he's only telling us what he plans to do and why—he's not physically doing it. We know his motives, yes, but knowing he "plans to shoot the zombie" is different from seeing him pull the trigger and save his life.

Look at the sentence again:

> ▶ Bob reached for the rifle to shoot the zombie.

It doesn't show Bob grabbing the rifle or shooting the zombie; it tells readers he *intends* to grab the rifle and *plans* to shoot the zombie. It's all explaining what Bob is going to do, not what he *actually* does.

Blows the mind a little, doesn't it?

A quick note about "for": When a character is "reaching for" or "heading for" something in a scene, the context and reason is usually obvious. If someone says good-bye and gets up, heading "for the door" is implied. Even if someone had no idea why someone was reaching or moving, looking at the situation and making a reasonable guess is usually enough to provide the necessary clues to understand the motive behind the action. Using "for" this way is taking *show, don't tell* to the extreme to make a point. Don't worry—no one is going to hit you with the telling stick for using "for" in your writing.

Let's take that told sentence and see what happens when we edit it to show.

The easiest (and most common) fix is to edit out the red flag words "for" and "to [verb]." When we do that, we get:

▶ Bob grabbed the rifle and shot the zombie.

This now shows, but showing doesn't improve the writing at all. It's boring, flat, and not a particularly entertaining or well-written sentence. So what went wrong with turning this from told to shown?

In this case, there's action implied with the motive "to shoot" that doesn't make it into the sentence when the motive is removed. It's clear the author intended to describe the shooting after telling readers what was coming. It basically says, "Hey, Bob grabbed that rifle and is going to shoot this zombie in a second, and it's going to be awesome." But we don't see any of that awesomeness dramatized. There's no "show" for the motive.

We've already learned how context can affect *show, don't tell,* so let's flesh this out a bit so we see more of the scene. Say the original snippet read like:

▶ An undead horror crashed through the door and into the hotel room. Bob reached for the rifle to shoot the zombie. The barrel flashed and a deafening bang shook the windows. He sighed. *Hasta la vista,* zombie.

More exciting, but still not great. It's a general, bland description of what's happening in the hotel room. The showing isn't making us feel any more connected to what's going on than the telling did. To fix this, we need to identify what's *really* going on in this paragraph and what we're trying to convey to readers. Let's analyze:

A zombie crashes into the room [An undead horror crashed through the door and into the hotel room]. *Because of that*, Bob decides to grab the rifle [reached for the rifle] *with the intent* to shoot it [to shoot the zombie]. The rifle fires [The barrel flashed and a deafening bang shook the windows]. Bob is pleased. [*Hasta la vista*, zombie.].

The only actions shown in this paragraph are the zombie crashing into the room and the rifle going off. Most of what Bob does is a tell saying what he plans to do. Only at the end does he sigh and think happy thoughts.

If we show Bob's actions as well, we get:

> ▶ An undead horror crashed through the door and into the hotel room. Bob snatched the rifle off the bed. The barrel flashed and a deafening bang shook the windows. He sighed. *Hasta la vista*, zombie.

Bob is now acting and that action is shown, but it reads even *more* like a list of events. We see Bob snatch the rifle, but it's disconnected from the shot. The writing is no better than the told sentence we started with. It's probably worse, because it's clunky and awkward without any sense of the character.

This is a good example of how telling sneaks into our writing, and why fixing told prose doesn't always make the prose better. Without *some* suggestion of motive, a list of actions feels just as detached and external as a tell. It *sounds* bad to our ears, and our writer's instinct knows we need that motive to make it work, so out come the tells.

The reason Bob acts is just as important as what he does, so let's show the motive this time:

> ▶ An undead horror crashed through the door and into the hotel room. *Aw crap, not again.* Bob snatched the rifle off the bed and aimed at the zombie's head, right between its bloodshot eyes. The barrel flashed and a deafening bang shook the windows. He sighed. *Hasta la vista*, zombie.

Now there's a smooth narrative flow from action to thought to decision to action. Putting the motive back in with the action personalizes the paragraph and shows a character experiencing a situation. The internalization shows Bob's reaction to the zombie crashing into the room, which spurs him to act. It's the reason he's motivated to grab the rifle and shoot. Aiming shows Bob's intention to shoot the zombie. His sighing and internal quip show his reaction to surviving.

The red flag words showed us where the problem was, but we had to imagine the scene and determine what was going on to improve the writing. Changing a few words didn't make the paragraph any better, because it wasn't about the text, but the amount of *information* being conveyed to readers. The event needed more to be understood and enjoyed.

Although showing frequently uses more words than telling to get the same idea across, we could have written this with fewer words and had a similar effect:

> ▶ A zombie crashed into the hotel room. *Aw crap, not again.* Bob snatched the rifle off the bed, aimed, and fired. *Hasta la vista*, zombie.

Of course, if this was a pivotal moment in the story, we could easily have expanded this into a longer scene.

How much is shown depends on what's needed at that moment in the novel, so don't feel you need to take every instance of told prose and flesh it out into multiple paragraphs. Expand what needs more, cut what isn't necessary, and strengthen what's weak. Sometimes, changing "to" to "and" is all you need to turn a sentence from told to shown.

Use the Right Word for the Job

Since one word can turn a told sentence into a shown one, choosing the right words for your novel is critical. But with so many words to choose from, it can be daunting to know which one will work best for your story. Strong nouns and verbs are a must, but even strong nouns can carry the wrong impressions and cause readers to make the wrong assumptions.

Are *your* words making the right first impression?

Several years ago in one of my workshops, I had the attendees try exercises to spark ideas about how to describe specific emotions from a particular point-of-view character. Some very interesting things surfaced as they read their samples out loud.

Certain words triggered certain assumptions. They showed, but they showed the wrong thing.

One exercise required drawing two cards—one from the "person" stack and one from the "emotion" stack. The task was to write a scene without using the word on either card and get the fellow attendees to guess the person and emotion based on the details provided in the scene.

Someone drew "optimistic criminal." When she read her scene, it was clear that the point-of-view character was a person who knew he was going to get away with whatever he was doing, but when the time came to identify the point-of-view character, everyone guessed law enforcement—even though the point-of-view character was clearly stealing.

What gave this impression?

One word.

The author had used the word "team" to describe the criminal's friends who were coming to help/aid/save him. It's an accurate word, but "team" evoked a partnership, law enforcement, military, basically the good guys. And "team" is what everyone picked up on despite all the great words that said "criminal."

Someone in the class suggested "crew" as an alternative, because "crew" has a criminal vibe (unless you're talking about boats, of course). If the point-of-view character had been waiting for his "crew," there would have been no doubt that he was a criminal.

Either word on its own can work in either situation, but combined with the other details in the scene, a picture emerged in the readers' minds. They made assumptions based on what was read, and it didn't matter that their assumptions were wrong. The author put those assumptions in there by the words she chose.

A word might have a certain definition, but if the most popular and widely used one is not what you mean, odds are readers will get the wrong idea.

One word *can* make a difference in how readers see a scene or a paragraph. When you're editing for told prose, pay particular attention to the words you use. Showing a scene won't help your story if the words you use show something different from what you intend. You want every word to draw your world and your story the way you see it.

Revise Red Flag Words

Over the years, I've discovered certain words associated with told prose—red flag words. These words frequently explain motives, throw off the natural stimulus/response order of events, and make emotional moments sound melodramatic. When I find one of these words in a manuscript, there's a high chance it's making a sentence feel told.

While not every instance of a red flag word is a problem, it is a good place to start if you receive feedback that you're telling and not showing. Simply search for each red flag word and edit as you see fit.

Although these red flag words will help you find told prose on a text level, much of spotting told prose is learning what to "listen" for. Told prose sounds flat and loses all sense of style or voice. Read enough of it and you'll develop an ear for hearing told prose when you come across it.

It's something that develops with time, exposure, and practice, so don't worry if it doesn't come to you right away. In this section, you'll learn a few shortcuts to help you develop your "telling ear" faster.

Hunting for and editing these words will take time—there's no way around that—but in the end, you'll have a much better story that shows instead of tells. Better still, you'll train yourself to identify and catch these troublemakers before they muck up your story.

As you go through these lists and search for these words, remember:

Just because a word is a red flag for telling doesn't mean you have to cut every instance of it from your writing (honestly, I can't stress this enough).

These are words that COULD indicate you're telling, not showing. It's up to you to decide if the word is doing what you want it to do, or if you can make the sentence stronger.

Like everything else, whatever serves the story is what's best. If something jars readers out of the narrative or makes them feel detached and disinterested, change it. If it doesn't and readers stay hooked and immersed in the story, you're golden.

Motivational Tells

A good guideline for revising motivational tells is to consider if the motive would be obvious to the narrator or not. Would an outside observer correctly assume the motive triggering an action by watching this character? If yes, having the narrator assign motive probably will not feel told. If no, then attributing motive likely will feel told.

If you can tell why someone is acting from sheer observation, attributing motive to the action is a reasonable assumption.

Red Flag Words for Motivational Tells: To [verb], decided, because, tried, when.

Let's take a closer look at these words and discuss options for revising them.

To [Verb]

"To [verb]" is one of the biggest telling offenders, and the one least likely to bother anybody. Since a high percentage of novels are written in past tense, it's assumed the narrator is relaying events after they've happened. It makes sense that the person telling the story knows why the other characters did what they did, so a minor point of view shift using "to [verb]" slides right by.

If the shift is larger and more obvious, or feels like author intrusion, showing the motive fixes the problem. We see this type of motivational tell problem more often in novels with tight points of view. In these novels, stating the motive of non-point-of-view characters can feel detached at best, or come across as a glaring point-of-view-shift error at worst.

If it's a minor point of view shift that tells motive of a non-point-of-view character, simply changing "to" to "and" usually fixes the problem.

For example:

- ▶ **Telling**: He reached over to brush the hair out of my eyes.

- ▶ **Showing**: He reached over and brushed the hair out of my eyes.

This changes it from "the intent to brush my hair" to "the action of brushing my hair."

If the "to [verb]" tell requires more, then look for words, thoughts, and action that suggest the "to [verb]" phrase.

For example:

- ▶ She moved to prevent Lisa from leaving the room.

Think about ways someone would act to prevent someone from leaving. They might:

- Dart in front of the door.

- Say, "You're not going anywhere."

- Shake their head as they move into that person's path.

- Draw that person's attention to something else, distracting them from moving.

Consider the person and how that character would perform that "to [verb]" task, and use those details to show.

- ▶ "Hey," she said, tugging on Lisa's shirt. Lisa turned away from the door. So far, so good.

We can see the narrator doesn't want Lisa looking at or standing near the door, but not exactly why. So the action is shown, and the mystery keeps it interesting. Why is the narrator keeping Lisa away from the door?

Decided

"Decided" is an important word, as it indicates where a character made a choice. Choices create plot and cause events in the novel to happen. These are vital moments for readers to be a part of, so telling here could keep them from getting lost in the tale.

▶ **Telling**: She decided he didn't need to be part of her life after all.

▶ **Showing**: "Get out." She heaved his suitcase out the door.

Consider what actions someone who made that decision would take in that situation. What would they do, think, or say?

Because

"Because" is a red flag word that you can almost always delete and not lose anything. It announces that the reason for something is about to be explained.

▶ **Telling**: Jane paused outside the room, because Bob was in there alone and she wasn't sure she wanted to talk to him right now.

Even just cutting "because" makes this more shown.

▶ **Showing**: Jane paused outside the room. Bob was in there alone and she wasn't sure she wanted to talk to him right now.

Using "because" makes it read like an explanation, but the line on its own could easily be Jane's internal thought.

To flesh this out even more, you could let Jane pause, act oddly and walk away, so readers can wonder why she doesn't want to be alone with Bob.

Tried

Characters try to do a lot of things in stories. They try to get up, they try to hide, they try to hold back tears. Sometimes the act of trying is valid, but a lot of times, what the writer really means is that they *do* something, not *try* to do something.

That doesn't mean every instance of "tried" needs to be cut from your manuscript, but it is worth taking a peek to make sure your character really is trying, and not doing.

▶ He tried to stand, grabbing the chair and dragging himself upright.

"Tried to" suggests failure. An attempt was made but it was unsuccessful. However, at the end of *this* sentence, the guy is standing. He didn't try, he did.

▶ He tried to sneak into the girls' locker room.

Based on this sentence, did he or did he not get into the locker room? You can't tell, but the "tried to" without any indication of success implies that he failed. You can almost hear the "but he got caught" at the end of it.

▶ She tried to smile.

This one's tricky because you don't know if she's standing there with a weird look on her face or if she isn't smiling at all. What does the "tried to" mean here? It's ambiguous because we only know the intent, not the outcome of this action.

"Tried" can indicate a personal struggle for the characters. In some cases it works fine, but in others it's accomplishing the opposite of what you might want.

▶ I tried not to squirm, tried not to think about the soldier's hands.

In this example, is she squirming or not? Again, you can't tell. It's clear she's thinking about the soldier's hands since she mentioned them, so "tried" (and thus failing not to think) works here. But for that first "tried"? It could go either way. She could be squirming, or standing still, or trying to stand still but twitching a little.

When evaluating "tried," ask yourself:

■ Are you intending to show the struggle, the failure, or the success?

■ Are you showing an action or a motivation?

■ .What is your character actually doing?

Clarifying "tried" will not only fix potential told areas, but will make the manuscript cleaner overall.

When

"When" not only keeps readers distanced from the point-of-view character, it usually puts the character's response *before* the stimulus, so readers see what Bob does before they know why he decided to do it. Seeing the result first takes all the fun out of a sentence.

> ▶ John yelped in surprise when his friends jumped out from behind the furniture at his birthday party.

There's no sense of surprise here, only a detached summary of what happened. It's a lot more fun to see the surprise.

> ▶ John opened the door and flicked on the light.
>
> "Surprise!" a chorus of voices cried.
>
> He yelped, backpedaling into the hall.

Readers see events in the order they happen, and can be surprised right along with John.

"When" is also a double-duty word found both in motive and stage direction tells. It can imply reasons a character acted, such as:

> ▶ When Bob saw the zombie, he ran for the cabin.

Or it can describe stage direction and explain how events occurred, such as:

> ▶ When the timer hit zero, the building exploded.

If it's explaining a personal reason for acting, it's a motivational tell. If it's describing how events unfolded, it's a stage direction tell.

To fix, put the action first, then let the characters react to it:

> ▶ A zombie lurched toward him. "Braaaiiinss!"
>
> Bob ran for the cabin.

In most cases, revising to put events in the correct order and dramatizing them will fix a "when" tell.

Emotional Tells

A good guideline for revising emotional tells is to consider the physical effects of the emotion you're trying to convey. Think about how someone experiencing that emotion would feel. What physical symptoms and sensations might they feel? What thoughts would go through their minds? In general, the tighter the point of view, the more important showing emotion becomes.

An observer should be able to look at the character and guess their emotional state by what they're doing, saying, or thinking.

Red Flag Words for Emotional Tells: In, with, felt.

Common Emotional Tell Situations: Overly self-aware characters.

Let's take a closer look at these words and discuss options for revising them.

In [emotion] or With [emotion]

"In [emotion]" and "with [emotion]" are as common as "to [verb]." They're fairly benign tells, but unlike "to [verb]," they're a missed opportunity to emotionally connect with readers. Making readers *feel* contributes to how much they'll enjoy a novel. If the emotions are explained and appear only on the surface, you risk never connecting with your readers.

For example:

▶ Chuck sighed with relief.

▶ The assassin dove through the window, knives glinting in the moonlight, and Lori screamed in fear.

Not only is the fear redundant in this example (screaming is usually caused by fear in this situation), it doesn't give any additional information or strengthen the verb, screamed.

▶ The assassin dove through the window, knives glinting in the moonlight. Lori screamed, her knees buckling beneath her.

Knees buckling is a good "fear" indicator. Better still, it shows how the sudden appearance of an assassin affects Lori on a physical level.

If this reads a little melodramatic to you, deleting the told phrase works just as well.

▶ Lori screamed.

If you've provided details and a reason for her to scream, readers won't need to be told it was "in fear." If you haven't, that's the place to start to revise this from told to shown. Make it clear why the character is having that emotion, and you don't need to explain it.

Felt

"Felt" is a common filter word, but it's a little different when it applies to emotions versus the senses. "Felt her heart breaking" is internal, while "Felt the wind on her face" is external. An emotional tell is internal, and "felt" tells *how* a character feels, not *what* she feels.

For example:

▶ Kim felt as if someone had ripped out her heart.

This is a lot of pain, but we don't *feel* Kim's hurt. "Felt" explains that she has pain, and it's bad, but shows no details or physical clues that would help readers also feel that pain. Consider how someone would feel if they'd been hurt in this fashion. Don't forget internal thoughts! Emotions are often expressed verbally.

▶ She couldn't breathe. A hollowness echoed in her chest.

▶ Moving was pointless. Living was pointless.

▶ *She'd pay for this.* Kim gripped the knife and pictured the hole she'd carve in that monster's chest.

Characters who "feel" emotions are typically those experiencing something profound or important to the plot or story. Put yourself in their heads and imagine what they would be feeling physically, what they'd think or say, and how that emotion would make them act or react.

Overly Self-Aware Characters

Some emotional tells don't have a red flag word to spot them—the characters are simply being too self-aware of how they feel. People don't think about the reasons for their emotions, they just have them—unless they're writing in their journals or crafting poetry.

For example, here's a point-of-view character who knows exactly what she's feeling and why:

> ▶ I wiped the sweat from my brow, fear from my narrow escape coursing through my veins.

It's unlikely someone would be thinking about what's coursing through her veins or why, especially after a narrow escape. She'd more likely think:

> ▶ Sweat dripped into my eyes and I wiped my face on my shirt. I got away. I can't believe I got away. I stumbled to a bench and collapsed, my legs trembling.

Here she notices how she feels, what she's thinking, how her body is reacting. It's looking outward *from* her skin, not inward *at* her skin. It doesn't explain why; it gives enough clues so readers can easily surmise, "Oh, she must be scared."

Avoid explaining why to readers, and show the results of that why instead. They'll figure out the why by what they see on the page.

A key thing to remember with emotional tells: Often, it's how a character reacts to an emotion that matters, not the sensations of the emotion itself. "Tears ran down his face" has been written thousands of times. "He stole her cat and vanished into the night" is a bit more unexpected.

Mental Tells

A good guideline for revising mental tells is to decide if you're explaining that a character had a thought, or if you want that thought to be part of the text. Does the character "know" going into the dark alley is dangerous, or does she see shadows and hear breathing that provides clues to this fact? Does he "realize" he can't live another day without his love, or are there physical and emotional symptoms that make him think such a thought?

Readers should be able to figure out what a character believes about her situation by what she thinks and how she acts.

Red Flag Words for Mental Tells: Knew, believed, realized, thought, prayed, wondered, hoped, considered.

Let's take a closer look at these words and discuss options for revising them.

Knew or Believed

"Knew" and "believed" appear when the author is about to butt in and explain. Often, what is "known" or "believed" steals all the suspense and mystery from the sentence, because it leaves nothing for readers to wonder about. It's also frequently paired with "because," not only explaining what's happening, but dumping in the reason *why* it's happening as well. When you find "knew/believed" and "because" in the same sentence, it's like a giant neon sign for told prose.

> ▶ Sally knew what was going on between Bob and Jane. It was so obvious.

It might be obvious to Sally and the author, but odds are readers aren't so well-informed. When you find "knew," look for clues in the text that the characters could have picked up on to "know" what they know. If there's nothing in the text itself that would trigger that assumption, add a detail or two that would.

> ▶ Sally believed Bob and Jane were having an affair. It was so obvious.

Consider what details might suggest an affair between Bob and Jane.

- Hushed whispering when they thought no one was looking

- Lingering glances or touches

- Sympathetic looks from others, pitying her

If Sally picks up on clues and "knows" or "believes" something, readers should be able to see those clues and make the same assumption, even if the clues are there to mislead them into making the *wrong* assumption.

Let's look at what happens when "because" gets involved:

▶ Sally knew what was going on between Bob and Jane, because Bob acted like a kid with a crush whenever he saw her.

The one benefit to a "knew, because" tell is that everything you need to show is right there. The "because" tells you how to make the reason shown. Sally "knows" this "because" of that. Simply add examples of Bob acting like a kid with a crush when he's around Jane, and Sally getting angry about it, and the situation is shown without ever needing this sentence.

Realized

"Realized" isn't a word we use when we realize something. We just do it. Unless the point-of-view character *is* referring to something he'd realized in the past, odds are this word will feel told.

"Realized" is the trickiest mental tell of them all, because sometimes, "realized" is the right word and it works as intended. But other times, it's used to explain how a point-of-view character came to a conclusion.

▶ A door creaked, and Bob realized he'd forgotten to lock the back door.

This tells me what Bob realized; it doesn't show him realizing it. The explanation also robs some of the excitement from, "a door creaked." Imagine someone talking over the tensest part of a movie. The music is building, something happens, and the guy next to you starts telling you why.

▶ A door creaked. Bob spun around, heart racing. Oh no, the back door!

We can now see the action that triggered the realization, and worry with Bob about what might have just come into the house.

Another potential problem with "realized" is that is can lessen the emotional impact of a key scene. If the whole point of the realization is to show a critical change in thought or worldview, stating it outright could steal the emotional importance from the moment.

▶ **Telling**: Bob realized he didn't have the heart to tell Jane no.

▶ **Showing**: He could refuse, but his throat tightened around the words. How could he tell *Jane* no? He'd rather cut off his left arm than hurt her.

Realization redundancy can also hurt your prose. If you show all the right details to "realize" the situation or thought, then you don't need to tack on a "realized" to make sure readers get it.

▶ Bob pulled the trigger. *Click*. He realized the gun was empty.

Yep, that's pretty obvious. Readers will see that without being told.

When you find "realize" in your text, think about how you intended it. Is it referring to something realized earlier, or is it the moment of realization? If it's happening at that moment in the story, look for ways that someone realizing something would act instead.

Thought

"Thought" falls smack in the middle between shown and told. If it's used as a dialogue tag, there's a good chance it feels told. Remember, every internal thought a point-of-view character has is something "she thought," so saying so is often redundant. But depending on the narrative distance, "she thought" might be as invisible as "she said."

For example:

▶ Maybe I'll go check out the new band at the Bronze, see what's what, I thought.

In a first-person point of view, adding "I thought" will likely feel told, because the narrative distance is so close. The narrator wouldn't tell readers she had a thought; she'd just think it.

- ▶ Maybe I'd go check out the new band down at the Bronze. See what's what.

This feels shown because it's how the character would think in her voice. But let's look how that subtly changes when we shift into third person.

- ▶ Lisa thought she'd go check out the new band down at the Bronze. See what was what.

Feels a little on the told side doesn't it? The "see what was what" helps, as that has some voice to it, but the first line feels distant. To make it feel more shown, let readers know this is her thought.

- ▶ Maybe she'd go check out the new band down at the Bronze. See what's what.

An easy way to show internal thoughts is to draw attention to the character's head before the thought. It's like a clue to readers that says, "I'm going into her head now."

- ▶ Lisa pulled her hair into a ponytail. She'd go check out the new band down at the Bronze. See what was what.

Most times "thought" can be eliminated if you simply show the thought itself, or cut the tag.

Prayed

"Prayed" is a great example of a red flag word that works better as a tell, because stopping the story to show the prayer would most likely bog it down. But if the prayer is short, you could show it.

- ▶ He vanished into the night, the shotgun in his hand, and she prayed he'd make it to the tower alive.

- ▶ He vanished into the night, the shotgun in his hand. *Please let him make it to the tower alive.*

Either line could easily end a scene or chapter.

However, if "prayed" is used as a tag, it can usually go.

▶ He vanished into the night, the shotgun in his hand. *Please let him make it to the tower alive, she prayed.*

Wondered and Hoped

"Wondered" and "hoped" are red flag words that could either be showing or telling, because we do think, "I wonder what's for dinner," and, "I hope it's something I like."

▶ Joey headed to the kitchen, wondering what was for dinner. He liked fish sticks and he hoped his mom had made those tonight.

It's not a terrible tell, but feel that distance? It feels like an outside narrator, not Joey. If you're using an outside or omniscient narrator, this probably works fine in your manuscript.

▶ Joey headed to the kitchen, wondering what was for dinner. Maybe Mom made fish sticks.

Very few readers would notice or be bothered by this. It flows smoothly and doesn't push readers away from the point-of-view character. But if you wanted a tighter point of view, you could get even closer:

▶ Joey headed to the kitchen. What was for dinner? Hopefully Mom made fish sticks.

The red flag words are gone, and the focus is fully on what Joey does (he heads to the kitchen) and thinks (What was for dinner? Hopefully Mom made fish sticks).

"Wondered" and "hoped" will work just fine in most sentences but like "thought," they're opportunities to tighten the point of view and flesh out the character. Removing them will allow you to show voice, because the character is wondering and hoping, the author isn't saying that they *are* wondering and hoping.

Considered

"Considered" is a lot like "thought." There are places where it's used as a verb, and it reads fine. But other times it's a dialogue tag or descriptive summary and it feels told.

> ▶ Bob wasn't sure about this. He considered his options. One: run out the back and hope for the best. Two: blast their way out the front door. Three: stay there and kill everything that came into the room.

This reads fine, but the "he considered his options" tells readers what Bob is doing, when the next three lines show him considering his options. Is the "he considered" line necessary? Maybe, maybe not. It's a style issue for the author to decide. It's an easy tell to fix, however:

> ▶ Bob wasn't sure about this. Wasn't like they had a lot of options, though. One: run out the back and hope for the best. Two: blast their way out the front door. Three: stay there and kill everything that came into the room.

Eliminate the "he considered" and this feels more shown and in Bob's head.

A rule of thumb on mental tells: If the mental tell word is used conversationally, as in "I thought I'd run out to the store," or "She'd hoped they'd make it back okay," then odds are it's working and showing, as it's either part of the internalization or dialogue.

If it's used as a dialogue tag or description of the action, there's a good chance it's telling. And remember that action can mean thinking and realizing as well—whatever "act" the character is taking.

Stage Direction Tells

A good guideline for revising stage direction tells is to consider where the narrator is when describing events. Is she inside the point-of-view character's head as these events unfold, or standing on the sidelines watching it happen? Is she relating events after they've happened or experiencing them at that moment? Keep in mind, even if the text is written in past tense, if the novel is happening as readers read it, and the point-of-view character has no prior knowledge of events, then it's still happening "at the moment."

Readers should be able to see the action unfold as it happens, and be able to understand what's going on through the descriptions provided.

Red Flag Words for Stage Direction Tells: When (directional), as, by, after, before, since.

Let's take a closer look at these words and discuss options for revising them.

When

One of the more obvious forms of telling is the "when" statement. These phrases slip into the prose because the author knows what happens and describes the scene with that knowledge. Problem is, they usually convey too much in the wrong sequence, so that "when" sucks all the show out of the sentence.

For example:

> ▶ But when she tried to run for the door, Bob stopped her.

The point-of-view character doesn't know Bob is going to stop her until he does (unless this is a retrospective novel). The "when" is outside watching the action, not inside the point-of-view character's head experiencing it. It also tells readers that something has happened before it has, which often robs the scene of its tension.

> ▶ She ran for the door and Bob stopped her.

A tiny change, but the second example is more active. The point-of-view character acts, and there's a response to that action—she runs, Bob stops her. Of course, we've seen how just making a sentence shown doesn't necessarily make it better, and this is another good example of that. Eliminating the "when" leaves the sentence sounding flat. Readers need to see the action:

> ▶ She bolted for the door. Bob lunged for her, arms out. His fingers raked the back of her shirt and grabbed the hem.
>
> "Gotcha!"

Showing the action as it happens picks up the pace and creates a more exciting scene.

With "when," try describing what the sentence is explaining. You usually have all the information you need right there, and it's just a matter of fleshing it out.

As

"As" can be a useful word, but it can work the same as "when" does to throw off the natural stimulus/response structure.

▶ Bob ran for the cabin as the zombie swung at his head.

On first glance, this looks perfectly fine, right? But look at the two pieces closer. "As" implies these two actions happen at the same time. Bob does X as the zombie does Y. But the zombie swinging at Bob's head is what *makes* him run for the cabin. Bob can't run at the same time the zombie is swinging, because he hasn't made the decision to run *until* the zombie swings. One note here: If the zombie has been attacking before this and the swing is one of several swings, then it's plausible Bob anticipates it coming and can run *as* it swings.

By and After

"By" and "after" are shortcut words that can jump the action and leave readers behind. They gloss over everything that happens between two points.

▶ Miguel left the office, but by the time he got to the restaurant, his blind date had left.

The problem with "by" in this example, as with most of stage direction tells, is that it forces you to tell readers the outcome of the action. They don't get to see anything that leads up to Miguel discovering his date had left, or any feelings he had about not getting there in time. The resolution to the goal (getting to the restaurant) is "his date had left," which leaves Miguel in a detached, not-really-part-of-the-scene place. It's harder to show his reaction and move the scene forward.

If the action really isn't important until this moment, using "by" can open a scene and catch up readers quickly.

> ▶ By the time Miguel got to the restaurant, his blind date had left. The maitre d threw him a pitying glance and suggested he try the house bourbon.

If "by" summarizes unnecessary action, it can usually stay. But if it skips steps vital to understanding the scene or lessens the emotional impact of the scene, it's probably telling.

> ▶ After he reached the summit, Hando took a well-deserved break.

This doesn't show Hando reaching the summit, just what he did afterward. If the journey there isn't important enough to describe, it's often better to pick up where the action starts.

> ▶ At the summit, Hando took a well-deserved break.

"By" and "after" have their uses, but they can easily slip into telling if you're not careful.

Before

"Before" sometimes falls into the same glossing-over trap as "by" and "after," but more often it creates ambiguity about what's happening in a scene (similarly to "tried").

> ▶ Brenda reached for the door before it hit her in the face.

Did the door hit her or not? "Before" refers to what the author knows is happening—the door swinging open toward Brenda, and her stopping it from hitting her in the face. But "before it hit her" suggests the door did hit her, and she failed to stop the impact. "Before" tells the outcome of something that *didn't* happen, which can confuse readers.

Fixing a "before" tell is fairly simple—be precise about what happens.

> ▶ Brenda stopped the door inches from her nose.

Minor edits will clear up most instances of ambiguous uses of "before."

Since

"Since" is the stage-direction version of "because." It explains the setup and the reasons for actions in the scene.

> ▶ Since Jane was already on top of the dumpster, Bob ran for the Suburban.

Bob doesn't look over and see Jane on the dumpster. It's explaining the reason he runs for the Suburban.

"Since" is also a red flag for infodumping, so be wary of any uses that preclude a lot of world building or character information.

> ▶ Lola slipped the surgical mask over her ears, since the air had been polluted by the chemical plant at the end of the block three years ago.

If you need to explain, odds are you're telling and there aren't enough details in the text to convey what you mean. Good stage direction describes how characters move around a scene without that explanation.

Descriptive Tells

A good guideline for revising descriptive tells is to consider who's doing the describing. Is it the character experiencing the world through his or her eyes, or the author explaining what the character experiences?

Every detail described should be a detail the character or narrator has a reason to comment on, and that comment should reflect who that character or narrator is.

Red Flag Words for Descriptive Tells: Saw, watched, heard, smelled, felt, could see, could hear, could feel, could smell, the sound of, seemed, looked.

Descriptive details are strongly influenced by narrative distance and point of view—probably more so than any other type of tell. Description is how authors tell readers what things look like. The smallest word can throw off how a paragraph reads, but because there's often nothing inherently wrong with it, we don't see where the problem lies.

This is where searching for the red flag words really pays off, allowing us to quickly find places where we're filtering or unintentionally adding narrative distance.

Let's look at descriptive tell so basic it appears in almost every book. (This is from my novel, *Darkfall*):

> ▶ We slipped out through the gates and onto the farm proper. Horses grazed in roped off corrals, with several wagons nearby. I saw a few carriages mixed in, proof that wealth didn't protect you from the Duke's soldiers.

The filter word "saw" is accurate, but since I'm describing what was seen, readers already know my protagonist, Nya, saw it. She's the point-of-view character after all. It doesn't add anything to the sentence and makes it feel told, as if Nya is listing what "she saw."

Eliminating the red flag word doesn't help much, though:

> ▶ We slipped out through the gates and onto the farm proper. Horses grazed in roped off corrals, with several wagons nearby. There were a few carriages mixed in, proof that wealth didn't protect you from the Duke's soldiers.

Again, a perfectly legitimate paragraph, but this feels just as flat and authorial with that "were" there, telling readers what was there instead of showing Nya seeing it. There's no real sense of *her* describing what she sees, and this could be any narrator describing this.

This is a perfect moment for a little voice and personality to bring it to life:

> ▶ We slipped out through the gates and onto the farm proper. Horses grazed in roped off corrals, with several wagons nearby. I even spotted a few carriages mixed in, proof that wealth didn't protect you from the Duke's soldiers.

These three words convey more than just what "was there." Although "spotted" is not that different from "saw," "spotted" implies Nya was *looking* for something, so she's actively engaged in what's going on and not just a casual observer. If she simply "saw" it, it feels like a passive detail. If she "spotted" it, it feels as though she was actively looking. "I even spotted" suggests the carriages might have been hidden or were unexpected finds, which suggests there's more to those carriages than meets the eye. It uses judgment from Nya, so it grounds it solidly in her point of view, as if she's proud she was able to spot those possibly hidden carriages.

It may not seem like much, but small edits can mean the difference between grabbing readers and having them skim through the scene. The words you use create the voice and put *your* style on the prose—it's not just a basic description anyone could have written.

Now that we've seen how a subtle word change can affect the text, let's take a closer look at filter words and descriptive red flag words and discuss options for revising them.

Could See, Feel, Hear, Smell

Some of the easiest told clean ups are sentences where your narrator "could [sense] something," and then go on to say what was sensed. This also includes the active versions of these verbs, such as, saw, felt, heard, smelled.

Some common "could [sense]" tells:

▶ Bob could see from the way Jane was acting she was upset.

▶ She could feel the smooth silk slide across her skin.

▶ A twig snapped. Bob turned around. He could hear a zombie lumbering through the bushes.

In most cases, specifying what is seen, felt, heard, or smelled will improve the sentence, showing without telling readers what was sensed.

▶ Jane threw a book at his head and stormed out of the room.

▶ Smooth silk caressed her skin.

▶ A twig snapped. Bob turned around. The bushes along the drive rattled as something large moved through them.

The Sound Of

The second cousin of "could hear" is "the sound of."

▶ The sound of a rifle echoed through the valley.

Using "the sound of" tells readers there's a sound, but it does nothing to show readers what that sound sounds like. Instead, try:

▶ The crack of a rifle shot echoed through the valley.

Small word changes, but doesn't this read stronger? Can't you hear that crack?

Seemed or Appeared

One strength of point of view is that you get to judge the world by your point-of-view characters' standards. They can assume incorrectly, have an unfair opinion, or just flat out be wrong. But sometimes ambiguity gets in there when you don't mean it to. "Seemed" can add ambiguity when you don't mean to.

When used well, "seemed" is a handy word that shows an assumption on the point-of-view character's part.

▶ Bob seemed happy, but his smile never wavered.

"Seemed" suggests that Bob is faking being happy. The point-of-view character senses something that feels off to her, and she's not sure she can take what she sees at face value. Bob *seems* happy, but she doesn't think he *is* happy.

Compare that to:

▶ Bob seemed happy, laughing and joking with all the kids.

The only word in this sentence that hints that Bob may not be happy is the word "seemed." If Bob really is happy, and his laughing and joking isn't an act, then "seemed" inadvertently misleads readers. If he isn't happy, there's nothing to suggest why not, which makes the point-of-view character feel a little shifty. Is she hiding information? Did readers miss something?

Of course, "seemed" is an effective word to use if the point-of-view character is making a guess about something she couldn't know purely by looking.

▶ The twisting path through the forest seemed safe.

When using "seemed," take a moment and consider if the point-of-view character really is assuming what she sees, or if she believes what she sees.

Questions about believing what a character sees often show up with "appeared."

▶ Bob appeared strong, with broad shoulders and biceps the size of canned hams.

Now, does Bob just have the appearance of a strong guy or is he really strong and does the point-of-view character agree with this statement? With "appeared" it's not clear. It's a judgment word that again suggests the assumption could be incorrect, yet someone with broad shoulders and big biceps probably is strong.

Now try something like:

▶ He appeared to be the charter pilot, with a jaunty cap and leather bomber jacket.

The details the point-of-view character describes could suggest he's a pilot or it could just be someone who dresses how the point-of-view character thinks a charter pilot would look. It's not clear that this person is the pilot, even though the point-of-view character *thinks* he might be. The uncertainty works.

When you use "appeared," if the description is dead on and can only be what it describes, perhaps cut the word "appeared."

Looked

"Looked" can be problematic because it could refer to what a character does, or how a character appears.

▶ Jane looked scared hiding behind the car, hands gripping the shotgun.

In this case, the point-of-view character could be describing what she sees, or she could be making an assumption. Does this sentence mean the woman hiding behind the car looks scared when she's really not, or is there a scared woman?

▶ Jane cowered behind the car, hands gripping the shotgun.

It's clear Jane is scared by the use of the word "cowered." There's no reason to suggest she might not be scared by using "looked."

If you *want* to suggest an opinion or judgment by the point-of-view character, "looked" is a great word to use.

▶ He looked like the kind of guy who would sell out his own mother for a cold beer.

You could easily continue the description, and thus show what the point-of-view character thinks a guy like that would look like, or leave it up to the reader's imagination. But there's no ambiguity about what the point-of-view character's opinion is here. It's all in the voice—one sounds like a detached description, the other like a character's opinion.

When using "looked," make sure you're not just introducing a description by saying you're about to describe something. Is there a chance it's not really what it looks like? Then "looked" works, same as "seemed." If it is clearly what it looks like, "looked" can send the wrong impression.

Unless the goal is to show what the point-of-view character sees might not be what it appears, words like seemed, appeared, and looked can change the tone or meaning of your sentence. It's not a bad idea to do a quick search to make sure they're saying what you want them to say.

Passive Tells

It's easy to assume all forms of passive writing or passive verbs are "bad" and must be avoided, but passive verbs and passive voice have their uses, same as any other element of writing. It's only when the passive words slide into unintentional telling that it becomes a problem.

Luckily, passive tells are one of the easier tells to fix—revising with active verbs eliminates the tell.

Red Flag Words for Passive Tells: Was [verb], will be, has been, by.

Let's take a closer look at the most common passive tell—the "was [verb]" sentence:

▶ Bob was bitten by the zombie.

Bob is the subject here, but Bob doesn't do anything, except maybe stand there like an idiot, and the zombie bites him, thus acting upon him. The passive verb is explaining (telling) what happened, not showing it in action. Fix the verb and we get:

▶ The zombie bit Bob.

This is a little boring, and to spice it up, we probably want the action to be something Bob does. To keep Bob as the main focus, we edit it so he's the subject of the sentence again:

▶ Bob screamed, jerking his leg from the zombie's mouth.

Passive writing doesn't always translate to telling, so take extra care when deciding if these red flag words are telling or not.

Adverbs and Telling

You've no doubt heard it over and over: Never use adverbs in your writing. Sound advice, but if you follow it to the extreme, you could miss out on their very useful properties.

As bad a reputation as adverbs have, they're handy during a first draft. They allow you to jot down how a character feels or how they say something without losing your momentum. You can keep writing, and go back and revise later.

They're also wonderfully helpful red flags that point out opportunities to revise and flesh out what your character is doing. They're like your brain telling you about the emotional state of your character, and pointing out a place you might want to examine further.

For example:

▶ I walked cautiously across the room to the back door.

Here, "cautiously" is doing the explaining, telling that this person is nervous in some way. You could find another word for "walked cautiously" like tiptoed, sneaked, or slipped, but that only solves the adverb problem. It doesn't do anything to capitalize on what your subconscious might be telling you. Instead, try looking deeper and showing someone *being* cautious in a way that helps characterize and further show the scene.

▶ I scanned the room, checking for tripwires, pressure plates, anything that looked like it might be a trap. Clear. I darted for the door.

This is interesting and tells you a lot more about what's going on, which probably saves you words somewhere else. Especially since there's a decent chance the description in that scene might be a little flat. If you had a better sense of the character's emotional state and what that character was doing, you probably wouldn't have used the adverb in the first place.

Adverb tells are used most often in dialogue. They're dropped in to show emotion or description without conveying what that emotion or description is:

▶ "I hate you," she said angrily.

In this instance, "angrily" doesn't say how the character speaks. Does she shout? Snarl? Spit? The adverb is vague and adds nothing to the sentence that readers didn't already assume by reading the dialogue. It's a pretty good guess saying, "I hate you" means she's angry.

Dramatizing the anger would show and thus make the scene more interesting. This character might bang her fist on a table, mutter snide comments under her breath, spit in someone's face, or even pull out a Sig Sauer nine mil and blow some guy's brains out. All of those would be more exciting than "angrily," which can mean something different to everyone who reads it.

By using an ambiguous adverb, not only are you falling into lazy writing, you're missing a great opportunity for characterization. The gal who would mutter snide comments is *not* the same gal who'd break out that Sig.

Now, let's look at a line like:

> ▶ "I hate you," she said softly.

Many people would swap out "softly" for whisper in this instance, but whisper isn't the same as speaking softly. You can speak softly and not whisper. "Softly" is an adverb that conveys something specific depending on the context in which it's used. It denotes tone as well as volume, attitude as much as forcefulness. What we pair with this adverb changes how we read it.

> ▶ She clenched her fists so tight her knuckles went white. "I hate you," she said softly. (Implies controlled anger.)

> ▶ She giggled, covering her mouth when the teacher turned their way and glared. "I hate you," she said softly. (Implies playfulness.)

> ▶ She kept the table between them, moving as he did around the edge. "I hate you," she said softly. (Implies fear or apprehension.)

All three sentences use the same adverb, but notice how each has a different feel to it based on what came before it. Anger. Playfulness. Fear. Can you replace the adverb with something else? Sure. You could even drop the tag entirely. Do you have to just because it contains an adverb? No. It all depends on what you want that line to convey to readers.

Adverbs work when showing the action would take more words than using the adverb, and that would gunk up the story. It could even shift focus to the wrong detail and confuse readers.

For example:

▶ She muttered incoherently.

This is clear and says what it needs to say. You could eliminate "incoherently" and dramatize it, but that might put too much focus on something that doesn't need that much focus.

▶ She muttered half-words that didn't make any sense.

Every writer will have their own preference here, but "incoherently" feels clearer to me in this instance than "half-words that didn't make any sense." I may not *want* readers trying to figure out what she's trying to say; I just want them to know she's not saying anything that makes sense. Making a point of *what* she's saying instead of *how* she's saying it could lead readers down the wrong path.

The reader/writer disconnect can happen at any time. Look at where you use adverbs and identify what you're trying to do with them. If what's in your head isn't making it to the page, you could wind up with a disconnect.

▶ "Oh, that's just wrong," Bob said angrily.

Here, the adverb is used to denote anger, but it makes readers decide what Bob's anger looks like and how he acts when he's angry. *You* might know Bob cracks jokes so he doesn't blow up, so you read his dialogue in a sarcastic tone, but readers might think Bob screams and yells, or maybe he gets quiet and dangerous. They could read that same line in different ways according to what "angrily" means to them.

Adverbs are effective placeholder words that let your subconscious know where you can craft stronger scenes and sentences. It's not always about replacing them with stronger words. Sometimes those adverbs are pinpointing an important aspect that would make the scene sing if you fleshed it out.

One Last Thought on Red Flag Words

When you're revising red flag words, take a step back and consider:

What are you trying to tell readers?

Once you pinpoint what's important and what needs to be conveyed, you'll be able to choose how to show that information. Look for ways to:

- Suggest motives through what a character does, says, or thinks.

- Show world-building rules through how those rules and details affect the character's actions.

- Show character backstory by choosing details and actions that had an influence on someone who lived through that history.

Make Details Come Alive

Showing dramatizes a scene and brings it to life, so the point of view and point-of-view characters are going to determine the right details for the scene. Showing a scene is wonderful, but the wrong words can give the wrong impression. "Showing" is only the first step.

Let's spend a little time exploring ways to describe scenes and how to choose the right details for the most impact.

Consider Who's Looking

Description that does nothing more than explain what something looks like sucks the life out of good text and can make it feel told, even when it's not. It's a statement of what the author knows is there, not how a character sees the world around her.

If the description is just what something looks like, it's a missed opportunity to evoke emotion, characterize, or create a mood.

For example:

▶ The early summer sky was a ruddy brownish pink.

There's nothing special about this line. It's not bad, but it's not a line that anyone is going to remember. But put it in the voice of a character, and show those same details through someone's eyes, and it becomes memorable:

▶ The early summer sky was the color of cat vomit (*Uglies*, by Scott Westerfeld).

One line tells us what color the sky is; the other shows us how the character feels about looking at that color sky. And that shows readers a whole different sky. The point-of-view character and her worldview change how she sees the sky and how she chooses to describe it.

Let's take a few random details in a scene and explore different ways to show the same scene. Rain, a clock, a restaurant, a window, pancakes, and an envelope:

> ▶ The rain poured down the window of the restaurant. Bob sat at the table, a stack of pancakes beside him. He stared at an envelope in his hands, while above him on the wall, a clocked ticked.

It's not bad, but it has no life to it. The details do nothing to tell us more than what this scene looks like. Is Bob happy? Sad? Do you care what might be in that envelope? Probably not.

Now, let's turn those same backdrop details into living details by thinking about:

Who's the point-of-view character: A Navy SEAL will look at a situation differently than a scared girl. Take the knowledge and attitude of your point-of-view character into account when showing a scene. Think about how they would describe something, not how you would.

> **SEAL:** The rain beat against the restaurant window like rounds from an Uzi. Bob sat at the table, back against the wall, a stack of uneaten pancakes beside him. He gripped the envelope tighter with every tick of the clock above him. New orders. Great.

> **Scared Girl:** Rain covered the window and blurred the outside world. Bobbi slouched at the table, her head barely higher than the stack of pancakes beside her. The envelope lay in her lap. She didn't want to touch it, let alone open it. She glanced at the clock and sighed. Running out of time.

Same details, but notice how different these are from the original bland backdrop? In these examples, there's a sense of who the point-of-view character is and what problem they might be facing.

Show why the point-of-view character is looking at those details:
Sometimes characters casually scan a room, sometimes they're looking
for something in particular, and sometimes they're looking for a way
to escape with their lives. The reasons for looking impact what they
see and how they feel about it. If your protagonist has no feelings at all
about what's around her, why are those details in the scene? Let's add a
little emotion to our scene:

> ▶ It was still raining. Why did it always rain when these things
> happened? Bob sat at the table, a stack of "have to order or
> get out" pancakes beside him. The open envelope lay next
> to it, a similar obligation written on the single, neatly folded
> page inside. He glanced out the window and sighed. Stuck
> in a stinking roadside restaurant today of all days. Figured.

Can you tell Bob has to do something he doesn't want to do? Do his pes-
simism and frustration come through?

Show which details are important to the point-of-view character:
People notice what's important to them. A girl obsessed with fashion
might notice what everyone is wearing, while a tired mom might not.
Spending time on details that mean nothing to your protagonist, or
seem weird for your protagonist to care about, could make the prose
feel told and knock readers out of the story. Let's change the emotion
and the details again:

> ▶ Rain pattered against the restaurant window like tiny, run-
> ning feet. Bob sat at the table, smiling a dumb, happy grin,
> the stack of pancakes beside him. He looked at the enve-
> lope again. How could one letter make everything so much
> better? The clock ticked and he hummed along with it. "It's
> mine, it's mine, it's mine."

Any guesses as to what might be in that letter? What's in the envelope
matters to Bob, and the rest of the details are just there. But here, they
don't feel "just there." Bob barely looking at them shows his preoccupa-
tion with the letter, and hints at what it says and his state of mind.

Show which details are important to the scene or story: Sometimes you need to put in a detail for plot reasons. Just tossing it in there might not be the best use of it, though. Too obvious a description or too much focus is like shining a light on it for readers. It practically screams, "Hey, pay attention here!" Maybe you want this, maybe you don't, or maybe you want the clue to hide in plain sight for a surprise later. If something needs to be seen, take a minute and think about how your point-of-view character might see it and how it can work *with* the scene, not just be *in* the scene.

> ▶ Bob slid into his usual booth by the window, watching the rain.
>
> "What's it gonna be today?" Sally asked.
>
> "I think I'll have the pancakes."
>
> "You got it, doll." She tucked her pen behind her ear and turned. A pale blue envelope fluttered out of her order pad and floated to the floor.
>
> "Hey, you dropped something." Bob bent over and picked it up. Postmarked Columbia.
>
> "What? Oh, that's not mine." Sally snatched the letter before he caught who it was addressed to. "But I'll toss it into the lost and found for you."
>
> "Uh, okay." He glanced at the clock. "Put a rush on those pancakes, would you? I've got court at one."

A longer passage, but it's obvious the envelope is going to be important. So is that postmark. Could it have something to do with Bob's court date? And does Sally know what it all means? The details help move the story and create interest in what's going on.

Show the tone, theme, or mood you want to achieve: If you're going for dark and creepy, describing bright and sunny could fight with your story, not help move it along. Showing the right mood details adds to the emotion of a scene. These details give you opportunities for similes and metaphors that flow seamlessly and evoke feelings in your point-of-view character. They can help illustrate your theme in subtle ways. They can foreshadow and even raise the tension by suggesting something foreboding or mysterious.

> ▶ Bob leaned against the wall, watching the rain wash away what was left of his life. A photographer walked over his body in the restaurant's doorway, shutter snapping the broken clock, the pancakes he'd never finish, the shattered window. The police paid more attention to the envelope clutched in his cold hand. Idiots.

I don't think anyone's going to mistake this for a comedy or a romance novel. The details are still the same, but they now suit the gritty, sad tone of a guy seeing his own dead body.

Details mean different things to different people. How you show those details to readers helps them better understand not only what's in the scene, but who's in it as well. The right detail can instantly pique a reader's interest and make them want to know more.

Don't just create backdrops. Make your descriptions count.

Let Your Characters Do the Work

We do a lot of work when we're developing a novel, and much of that research and planning goes into the text. When we do it well, it shows the story and readers see great writing. When we don't, they see infodumps and backstory and a lot of explaining how things work.

But we have allies to prevent such telling—our characters.

Letting *them* do the work allows us to show everything we need to without dumping all that told information into the book.

Let's look at ways to show infodumps and backstory without bogging the story down or falling into told prose.

Character Voice: Your "Get Out of Tell Free" Card

Here's the secret of *show, don't tell*: You can write pretty much anything you want to as long as it's in the character's voice. Put a little attitude into it, and it sounds like the character, not the author.

It's the characters' job to convey information to readers. They're the guides, the narrators, the camera lenses that allow readers to peek into the story world they inhabit and the adventure the novel is taking them on. Since it's a story, readers expect the characters to tell them that story. Telling becomes bothersome only when it pulls readers *out* of the story.

One common "tell, not show" problem is conveying world building information—the classic infodump. You have important information to share with readers and you can't show it.

When information that's important for readers to know to understand the story is not something that could easily come out in casual conversation, then telling *can* work. Let's look at a paragraph from my fantasy novel, *The Shifter*:

> ▶ Both paled when I mentioned the Luminary. We got a new one every year, like some rite of passage the Duke's Healers had to go through to prove their worth. The new Luminary was Baseeri of course, and like all Baseeri who held positions that should have been held by Gevegians, no one liked him. He'd only been here a few months, but already everyone feared him. He ran the League without compassion, and if you crossed him, you didn't stand a chance at getting healed if you needed it. You or your family.

This is Nya talking about something that impacts her life—the Luminary and the Baseeri who are occupying her city. It tells readers all about the Luminary and why he's there, but it doesn't feel like the story stopped to lecture readers because it's full of her personal attitude about the situation.

Putting it in Nya's voice makes it feel as though Nya is getting on her soapbox to rant about something she thinks is unfair in her world and doesn't like. It's in her head, showing her opinions as she thinks about something that matters to her. It flows with the rest of the narrative and says just as much about Nya as a character as it does about the world mechanics. It tells, but it tells readers something they want to know.

Let's take out her voice and dump this same information:

> ▶ The two boys paled when I mentioned the Luminary, the leader of the Healers' League. He'd only held the position a few months. The Duke sent a new person every year from Baseer, unwilling to trust native Gevegians in the position. The Gevegians didn't like him, but they feared him because he ran the League without compassion, and crossing him meant neither you, nor anyone in your family, would be healed if you needed it.

Feels like a big ol' explanation, doesn't it? It's information without soul—flat, boring details dumped into the text. It explains the situation, but not in any way that readers would care about. This is the author, not Nya.

Voice lets you get away with a lot. It turns whatever you're writing into a character experiencing it. And showing is all about feeling like you're there with the characters having the same experience.

Show Your Infodumps

When characters convey information, they can do it in several ways: They can dump the information into the story (the classic infodump tell), they can have another character talk about it (a potential infodump-as-dialogue tell, or a shown response to a character question), or they can observe their fellow characters in the scene and figure it out from what they see (showing the details in the background).

Imagine you're at a party and someone walks up to you and starts telling you all about the neighborhood and who was arrested and how many apartments were broken into last month. You didn't ask for this information, you don't care about this information, and you have no idea why someone is telling you this information.

Now imagine you're speaking with someone and you mention how much you like the apartment. You ask the hostess's neighbor how he likes living in that building. He tells you the same information, but now, you're listening because you wanted to know it.

Next, imagine you're at that same party, and you notice guests are leaving much earlier than people normally do at a party. You're worried you'll look foolish if you come right out and ask, so you start eavesdropping, trying to figure out what's going on. You hear people say, "I'd better head out before it gets dark," and, "I'd stay longer, but I forgot my mace." You start looking around and notice heavy locks on the doors and windows, and a state-of-the-art alarm system. It's not long before you figure out this isn't the safest neighborhood.

All three examples convey "this is a bad neighborhood" to readers. The first dumps information readers don't care about, so it'll feel told. The second offers information readers wanted to know, so even if it feels a little told, readers won't care. The third puts all the pertinent details in plain sight and lets readers figure it out by looking at the scene.

Examples two and three use the characters and what's happening in the scene to convey that information to readers. One shows more than the other, but they both work without stopping the story and boring the reader.

Having characters react to, or interact with, the world around them is one of the best ways to slip in an infodump without readers noticing. The information might be learned through something a character says or does, or an example of that information in action.

Infodumps that feel shown:

Stay in the point-of-view character's voice and worldview: It's not you explaining details, it's the characters musing about the world or history. It's information that matters to the characters and they have an opinion—often a strong one—about whatever detail or information they're talking about.

Trigger the information naturally by what's in that scene: Something in the scene triggers thinking about or mentioning the information. It might be something seen or heard by the characters, a detail that triggers a memory, or something important that needs to be considered for actions in the scene to work.

Keep the information relevant to the goals of the scene: Use information that influences what's going on in the scene at that moment. It might be information the point-of-view character is weighing in order to make a choice, it might affect the plan to achieve the scene goal, it might help illustrate the stakes, or it could provide the motivation for the protagonist to act.

Keep it short so readers aren't overwhelmed with information: Infodumps longer than a paragraph are more noticeable, so it's best to use them only when absolutely necessary. Shorter bits of information dropped in here and there are less obvious and are absorbed into the background as readers read the scene. A line of information written in the character's voice as she offers her opinion about the world reads as smooth as any other line of narrative.

Do more than just dump information: The best infodumps say just as much about the character as they do the information they're dumping. Readers learn about a character's personality, ethics, morality, views, and feelings about the world that character lives in based on how information is conveyed.

For example, a frustrated tirade about the homeless bringing property values down and creating crime could show an intolerant character brought up in privilege. Change that tirade to a sympathetic plea for compassion, and the character becomes someone who champions the poor and cares about her fellow citizens. Shift it to a pragmatic view of living on the streets, and someone who was once homeless and understands what it means to have nowhere else to go appears.

The more an infodump reflects the views of the character relaying the information, the more invisible it will become, and the more shown it will feel.

Show Your Backstory

How many times a day do you think about your past? Or bring up painful topics you're trying hard to avoid? Odds are, not very often, but told backstory has our characters doing it all the time.

Readers don't *want* to know everything about a character's past right away. Tell them too much too fast, and there's nothing for them to discover as the story unfolds. Readers want to be surprised. They want to wonder why your hero is scared of bright sunlight (when he's clearly not a vampire). They want to ponder the puzzle of that odd-shaped scar on your heroine's shoulder. They want to see if they can figure out who a character really is before it's revealed.

Letting your characters show their backstories gives readers all the clues they need, without giving anything away.

Here are things to consider when showing your backstory:

Put it in the background: If you want to tell readers about your protagonist's terrible past— and how he spent nine years underground in a Boramese prison—think of the things that might have affected him *because* of that experience. How might that history change his behavior in the scene? Is he extra sensitive to the light? Claustrophobic? Very good at getting around when he can't see well? By slipping in details as they become relevant to the scene, you can show the backstory and flesh out the character without stopping the story. Better still, you leave enough tantalizing hints that readers eventually *want* to know the whole story.

It's not about the character's history: Backstory isn't about the character's history; it's about the experiences that shaped their lives and made them act the way they do. Backstory affecting motivation feels natural because it has a place in the scene. You want to mention the history that's *driving* the character to act, not just random moments that happened in the past. Pick what's important both to the character and to the story itself and use *those* details.

To determine what backstory to show, ask:

How does the backstory affect the current scene goal? The character will use skills and behaviors learned over the course of his life to achieve his goals. Sometimes he'll reflect on where and how he learned it; other times he'll just use it and leave readers curious about it.

Were any of the scene's characters involved in the detail you want to show? If so, what was their role? How do they feel about it now? How does it motivate their actions and choices in the current scene or story as a whole? If they're not playing a role in the scene, why add backstory about them?

How does the point-of-view character feel about the backstory detail? The character who brags about past deeds is different from the one who downplays his achievements. Tight-lipped characters who exhibit intriguing skills or knowledge are compelling to readers. These characters tease readers with backstories full of possibilities, and the more hints readers see, the more they'll want to know the whole truth.

Sometimes discovering a character's backstory is a major part of the plot. If your point-of-view character is trying to figure out his history, anything he remembers could be important to the story. What does he know? What does he *think* he knows, but has wrong? Is he searching for answers, but uncovers something totally unexpected about his past? Or the reverse might be true—he's trying to *hide* a past he's ashamed of or knows is dangerous to those he cares about.

The past is a part of life, and everybody has one. In fiction though, that past isn't always relevant, even if it is interesting. Stopping to explain a character's history tends to bog a story down. But with a little forethought and revision (okay, sometimes a lot of revision), you can make your backstory flow seamlessly with the rest of your prose.

Common Trouble Spots

All told prose is not created equal, and some aspects are harder to show than others. Let's wrap things up with a closer look at handling four common trouble spots for told prose.

Showing a Character's Age

In some novels, age doesn't matter. Readers can usually assume the characters are about the same age as they are and it still tracks.

Other novels read differently depending on the age of the character. Imagine how a young adult novel would read if you suddenly made the protagonist thirty. Nothing would feel right and readers would likely assume that the author had lost her mind.

Getting a character's age into the story could be as easy as putting it on the cover blurb, such as, "Fifteen-year-old Nya does cool stuff," but you can't count on readers reading that or remembering it when they start the novel. Sometimes you need to mention it in the opening scene, but stating it can feel awkward, especially if you're writing a first-person point of view.

> ▶ I stood at the bus stop with my fellow sixteen-year-olds.

Um...yeah. What teen talks like that? It even sounds awkward coming from an adult.

> ▶ I stood around the water cooler, a thirty-three-year-old woman chatting with other thirty-somethings.

People don't think of their age in this way, but they do think about it and talk about it. All you need to do is find ways that flow naturally into the scene and still get that age across.

Three Ways to Show a Character's Age

Just say it: Age comes up in conversations, and when it does, it makes sense for a character to share how old she is. If your novel has a conversation where this flows naturally, this is a perfect place to get that information across. If you don't have a scene like this, then don't force it. It's much better to have one slightly awkward sentence with age mentioned than a very awkward scene trying to slip age in.

Ways you might show your character's age:

> ▶ "Hey, birthday girl," Bob said, grinning. "The big 4-0. Feeling old yet?"

> ▶ "I'm sixteen, Mom, I'm not a kid anymore."

> ▶ Lila snorted and toasted with her glass. "Hon, I'm eighty-three. It won't be the bourbon that gets me."

Just think it: A character can think to herself about her age as well, and sometimes an internal thought feels more natural, especially if the character is chiding herself. A character can also refer to her age in an offhand way that shows a passage of time.

Ways a character might think about age:

- ▶ I wasn't sure which saint covered luck, but I must've snubbed her big at some point in my fifteen years.

- ▶ Who was she kidding? She was thirty, not thirteen. This was no way to act around a man.

- ▶ Bob giggled and shoved the grenades into his pocket. Even at forty-one, grenades were something to get excited about.

Just suggest it: If stating the age outright won't work or feels awkward no matter what you do, try leaving clues that *suggest* the age of the character. Location can play a big role, as can clothing or accessories. Certain ages also come with traits that place the character in the correct age group, even if the exact age is still uncertain.

Showing age through the location:

- ▶ Lila walked up the steps of Ridgemont High, her lesson planner tight in her arms. (adult teacher)

- ▶ Lila walked up the steps of Ridgemont, waving at her BFF. (teen)

Showing age through clothing and accessories:

- ▶ Luis pulled his scrubs off and tossed them into his locker. (adult)

- ▶ Luis balled up his varsity jersey and chucked a perfect three-pointer into the hamper from the bathroom. (teen)

Showing age through miscellaneous details:

- ▶ Marla kicked off her shoes and flipped through the mail. Bills, more bills, credit card applications. (adult)

- ▶ Marla slipped her homework into her backpack. (teen)

Showing age through comparison:

- ▶ She looked better at fifty-three than I did at thirty-seven. (adult)

► The new kids looked a few years older than me, maybe old enough to drive. (teen)

A combination of details often works well to ensure the right age is being shown. It's possible for a teen to flip through the mail and see bills, just as a mom going back to school can put her homework into her backpack. That's why it's so important to...

Show the Context: What is going on around the character influences how readers will view that character. How the point-of-view character views the world will also influence readers. If the character is an adult, she'll see and interact with the world as an adult would, same as a kid or a teen would interact with their world, and they'd all do it differently.

Let's see how the same situation with different context and details changes how old the character feels:

► Lila walked up the steps of Ridgemont High. A group of students raced past, barely giving her a glance, but never getting too close. Would any of them be in her class? The students barreled past another boy and knocked him over. They laughed and kept on going. She took a deep breath. Jerks. Hopefully, they *weren't* in her class.

► Lila walked up the steps of Ridgemont High. A pack of guys raced past, barely giving her a glance, but never got too close. Would any of them be in her class? They barreled past a geeky guy and knocked him over, but just laughed and kept on going. She took a deep breath. Hopefully, they weren't in *her* class.

► Lila walked up the steps of Ridgemont High. A group of male students raced past without looking over, staying just out of range. Would any of them be in her class? The future delinquents barreled past another boy and knocked him over. They laughed and kept on going. She took a deep breath. They'd *better* be in her class.

There's a different attitude and voice in each of these paragraphs. What can we assume from what's written about the ages of these characters?

The first feels like a young teacher starting school. Clues such as, "students" and "another boy" suggest she's an adult looking at teens or kids, and "her class" suggests ownership of that class. Her concern over difficult students being in her class also suggests a younger, more unsure adult.

The second feels like a teen on her first day of school. Phrases such as, "pack of guys" and "geeky guy" are how a teen refers to her peers. Her wish that the jerks aren't in her class feels more teen in this context.

The third feels like an adult, but not young. Clues such as, "male students" and "future delinquents" suggest someone older and more cynical, as does the hope that these boys *are* in her class, so she can straighten them out or teach them a lesson.

It doesn't take much to drop enough hints that suggest how old a character is or what group she belongs in. A few words here and there is often all it takes to show age.

Showing Emotions

When showing emotions, it helps to put yourself in your point-of-view character's shoes and describe what she feels, sees, and does. Instead of saying, "Jane was scared," you'd show the results and outward signs of that fear.

If the emotion needs to be carried over a long scene, try spacing out the physical details so the reader can see the point-of-view character is feeling X emotion, and then slip in little reminders as the scene unfolds. If it's fear, the point-of-view character might start out with a racing heart, get the shakes later on, and wipe sweat from her brow after that. Avoid having her feel all three at once unless the scene calls for it, such as, if she's having a stressful "holy cow" breakdown moment or you want that heavy dose of emotion.

Also consider more subtle ways to show fear. A person acts differently when she's scared, and her reactions and thoughts will reflect that. She might constantly look around, or jump at sounds, or question everyone she sees and worry they're coming after her. She might grab a weapon and hold it tight, or put her back to a wall. She might pull her hair forward and hide behind it so no one can see her face.

She might also think about the stakes or what she has to lose. Worrying about being thrown in jail can show fear just as well as shaky hands. She might even talk to herself: *Don't see me, please don't see me.*

Mixing all of these elements into a scene helps space out the emotional details so you're not heaping them on readers all at once. Plus, if you save some details, you have the freedom to do a little more if the emotions get stronger later.

If the emotion *does* get stronger, it's often because the stakes have increased. This is a great time to use internalization or even dialogue to show what the point-of-view character is thinking. Make that emotion personal to her and not just an external feeling, and that'll help tweak those emotional stakes as well as the external stakes.

We fall more into telling when we rely on explanations to convey emotions and do nothing in the text to back it up.

Showing Sounds

There are lots of options for describing sounds, from a basic description, to a specific detail, to a judgmental observation. What you use is up to you, and you can vary it as much as you'd like.

Option One: He heard a rifle shot, followed by a scream (far narrative distance).

Option Two: Someone screamed, then a rifle shot echoed across the valley (medium or close narrative distance).

Option Three: Someone screamed. *Bang!* Bob tensed. Was that a rifle? (tight narrative distance).

Which one you use depends on what else is in the text or how often you use a particular style—for example, if all of your sounds are written as "she heard X" or "Sound, and then description" it could feel repetitious. Mix and match the sentence styles and use what serves the scene best.

Imagine what sounds your character might hear:

▶ Footsteps tapped away, getting softer.

▶ A chair squeaked, cloth rustled, and a soft thud, like a body falling to the floor.

▶ Their voices faded.

Sometimes your narrator isn't sure what she hears, and she makes assumptions about the sounds:

▶ Metal scraped across stone. Chains?

▶ Footsteps tapped away, getting softer. A thud, like a door closing, then nothing. He sighed. They were gone.

Words such as probably, like, as if, etc. state that the narrator is *assuming* something about what's heard.

It's also fun when your point-of-view character has enough details about the scene or setting to make an assumption. The descriptions read as if the character is trying to put the pieces together based on the information she knows.

▶ Wood creaked and a wave of cinnamon washed over me, probably from the kitchens.

This works best if you've already established the details your narrator is assuming. If you've never mentioned kitchens, it'll probably make your readers think, "Huh? What kitchens?" But if you've already seen or mentioned the kitchens in the story, it makes sense to refer to them.

You can also let your point-of-view character internalize what she thinks:

▶ Something large thumped in the other room. Jane tensed. A zombie? Sounded too loud to be a book.

This is a good example of where "sound" fits in very well. It's not the point-of-view character telling you there's a sound, it's her making an assumption *about* a sound.

You can also choose verbs that imply sound, using onomatopoeia or sound-evoking words:

▶ Waves sighed against the canal walls and hissed through the reeds growing along the boat launching ramp.

"Sighed" and "hissed" sound like water and conjure up the sounds of waves. "Swished" is another good one that implies a water sound.

▶ It (chair) crashed against the wall and clattered to the floor.

I just love "clattered." There's something about that word that screams "hard, repetitive bangs."

Like any descriptive detail, strong, specific words add so much to the sound you're describing.

Showing Tone and Mood

Setting the right tone can go a long way to showing readers your story. It's like the scary music in horror movies. With the sound on, the scene makes you nervous, so you jump when things happen, and your reactions enhance the overall experience. Turn the sound off and the scene isn't scary anymore.

The words you choose to show a scene are just like that music. Generic words that apply to any situation do little to create a mood. Common or clichéd words and imagery give the sense that readers have seen this before, so they know how it's likely to play out. Even if you *do* surprise them with what happens, odds are the anticipation of that surprise was lacking, so you miss out on the emotional punch.

If all you do is describe with accurate, yet generic words, then you miss opportunities to create emotional responses in your readers. You want them to feel the mood as if it were background music.

For example, there's a wonderful moment in the beginning of *Pirates of the Caribbean* where Captain Jack Sparrow is standing in the crow's nest as his ship pulls into port. It has a strong adventure feel—the mighty pirate surveying the land. Then, as the camera pulls away, you see his ship is sinking and it goes under just as he reaches the dock and steps off.

It's silly, it's comical, and it immediately sets the tone for the rest of the movie.

That first scene is over the top, but the creators of the movie want you to know that you can't really take anything very seriously, so hang on and enjoy the ride. It's all about fun. It's not a realistic look at pirates. You know what you're going to get after that, so anytime they get a little silly you just roll with it.

You can infuse your writing the same way.

Use imagery: If you wanted to show "tragic, yet hopeful," you'd think about images that convey hope and overlay them on tragedy. Flowers blooming in garbage. Kids playing in the ruins of a bombed-out apartment building. Sunbeams breaking through the dark clouds. Determination on someone's face.

Use specific words: Think about the words associated with the emotion you want to create. Crying is often about sadness, yet people also cry when they're happy. Crying and smiling sets a mood that's different from crying and frowning. You can juxtapose emotional keywords so they evoke the tone and mood you want.

Use the right sentence rhythm: Snappy banter is often fast-paced, short sentences, with little or no exposition or tags with the dialogue. It's light, funny, playful, and it feels that way. Anger is often portrayed with choppy sentences, and sudden starts and stops as people yell, then pause to think and yell again. Sadness is often shown with longer, slower sentences and lots of internalization. Consider the beats of the words, same as you would when writing poetry. Ending on a downbeat can signify sadness, while an upbeat can indicate happiness.

Use your characters: Your characters' thoughts and feelings also help set a tone. No matter how serious a situation is, if the point-of-view character is flippant and blows it off, it won't feel very serious, just as a character being overly dramatic in a situation that clearly doesn't call for it can feel melodramatic. If the character feels one way, and the rest of the scene backs that up, then you can help create that same feeling in your readers.

Let's say you wanted to get across a tense, suspenseful, "anything might happen at any second" tone—a guy walking across a courtyard who thinks someone is following him. You might write:

> ▶ Bob walked across the courtyard, nervously looking over his shoulder at every noise. He knew someone was back there. He could feel it in the twisting pit of his stomach.

Bob is nervous, but do you *feel* it? Probably not, because the word choices here tell more than they show, and they aren't helping set the tone of "nervous and scared."

Let's break it down:

> ▶ Bob walked across the courtyard, nervously looking over his shoulder at every noise. He knew someone was back there, he could feel it in the twisting pit of his stomach.

"**Walked**" does nothing to set tone because it's generic. It also doesn't suggest something is wrong.

"**Nervously looking**" tells us how he's looking, which distances us from the action. It's an adverb that relies on the reader to bring the details.

"**At every noise**" is also generic and does nothing to set the scene. What noises?

"**Knew someone was back there**" tells us what Bob knows, but does nothing to show readers or make *them* worry that someone is back there.

"**Feel**" tells, though "**twisting pit of his stomach**" has a nice vibe. However, it's a common way to show apprehension, so readers aren't likely to feel any real emotion from that.

Let's swap out a few words and see how the tone changes:

> ▶ Bob crept across the courtyard, glancing over his shoulder every few steps. His gut said someone was back there, and the twisting pit in his stomach was never wrong.

It might not win any awards, but it's better, showing the nervousness and increasing the tension.

"**Crept**" suggests he's sneaking or trying to be quiet, which implies he doesn't want anyone to hear or see him. People with nothing to worry about don't creep, so it immediately suggests intent.

"**Glancing over his shoulder**" is what nervous people do. It shows his nervousness and lets readers figure out the reasons why.

"**His gut said someone was back there**" becomes an internal thought, which puts readers more in Bob's head and thus more in the scene.

Same with the "**twisting pit in his stomach.**" Instead of a tired cliché, it's something Bob relies on to keep him out of danger, reinforcing the "**his gut said.**"

For a different approach, let's toss out the common elements and go for unexpected word choices and imagery:

> ▶ Bob slowed. Sunlight filled the courtyard ahead, chasing away the shadows and exposing every potential piece of cover. No way anyone could hide out there, but that applied to him as well as whoever was behind him. *If* anyone was. Crap.

These details create a different tone for the situation, don't they?

"**Slowed**" is the opposite of what most people would do if they thought they were being followed. It makes you wonder why he does it.

The idea that sunlight exposes things contrasts the sense of the shadowy lurker. What might be seen in the light? Is this setting up a reveal?

"**Potential piece of cover**" suggests training on Bob's part, which implies he's not just a random guy, so the person *following* him might not be either.

"**No way anyone could hide**" suggests he's already thinking of a plan, and that he sees the pros and cons of the location ahead as it pertains to his situation.

"***If* anyone was**" says he's not sure, creating a nice contrast to the sunny, "everything is okay up here" imagery of the bright courtyard.

"**Crap**" shows he's not happy about that and doesn't trust it.

Unusual word choices change the situation. Instead of a nervous guy walking across a courtyard, we now see a worried guy who recognizes danger ahead and is trying to figure out how to face that danger. There are also enough hints that indicate something is about to go down and it might not be what readers expect.

Think about what your point-of-view characters would see and how they'd interpret it. Choose words that create the mood or tone you want readers to feel, and show them things they haven't seen a hundred times before. Don't go for the easy or familiar. Unfamiliarity creates uncertainty, and uncertainty leads to anticipation. Once you have that, you have the reader wondering what will happen next.

Time to Show!

Congratulations! You made it.

Show, don't tell is a concept that has thwarted many a writer, and I hope you now have a much better understanding of it. Take what you've learned here and put it to work in your writing. Craft the scenes you imagine and bring your story to life for your readers..

I hope you've enjoyed my ridiculously in-depth look at *show, don't tell*. If you've found this book helpful, please share with friends or leave reviews on your favorite sites.

Most of all, best of luck and good writing!

Janice Hardy
September 2016

Appendix

Quick-check list of red flag words for easy manuscript review.

Common Red Flag Words

▶ **Common self-aware red flag words:** knew, realized, felt, thought. Not every instance will be a problem, but it's a good place to start the search.

▶ **Common stimulus/response red flag words:** when, as, before. Revise as needed so the stimulus comes first, then the character reaction.

▶ **Common telling red flag words:** when, as, to [verb], which, because, to be verbs. These are often found in told prose.

▶ **Common stage direction red flag words:** as, while, when, as. These often connect multiple actions in one long and confusing chain.

▶ **Common motivational red flag words:** to [action], when, as, while, causing, making, because.

▶ **Common emotional red flag words:** in [emotion], with [feeling].

▶ **Common descriptive red flag words and phrases:** realize, could see, the sound of, the feel of, the smell of, tried to, trying, in order to, to make.

▶ **Common passive red flag words:** to be verbs—is, am, are, was, were, be, have, had, has, do, does, did, has been, have been, had been, will be, will have been, being.

▶ **Common mental red flag words:** realized, thought, wondered, hoped, considered, prayed.

Thanks!

Thank you for reading *Understanding Show, Don't Tell (And* Really *Getting It)*, the first book in my Skill Builders series I hope you found it useful!

- Reviews help other readers find books. I appreciate all reviews, whether positive or negative.

- If you enjoyed this book, look for the other book in my Skill Builders series, *Understanding Conflict (And What It* Really *Means)*, available in paperback and e-book.

- Books in my Foundations of Fiction series include *Plotting Your Novel: Ideas and Structure* and the *Plotting Your Novel Workbook* and my Revising Your Novel series: *Fixing Your Character & Point-of-View Problems, Fixing Your Plot & Story Structure Problems,* and *Fixing Your Setting & Description Problems,* available in paperback and e-book.

- I even write fantasy adventures for teens and adults. My teen novels include The Healing Wars trilogy: *The Shifter, Blue Fire,* and *Darkfall* from Balzer+Bray/HarperCollins, available in paperback, e-book, and audio book formats. As J.T. Hardy, I write fantasy novels for adults, available in paperback and e-book formats.

- **Would you like more writing tips and advice?** Visit my writing site, Fiction University at Fiction-University.com, or follow me on Twitter at @Janice_Hardy.

- **Want to stay updated on future books, workshop, or events?** Subscribe to my newsletter. As a thank you, you'll receive my book, *25 Ways to Strengthen Your Writing Right Now.*

More from Janice Hardy

Award-winning author Janice Hardy (and founder of the popular writing site, Fiction University) takes you inside the writing process to show you how to craft compelling fiction: In her Foundations of Fiction series, she guides you through plotting, developing, and revising a novel. In her Skill Builders series, she uses in-depth analysis and easy-to-understand examples to examine the most common craft questions writers struggle with.

Understanding Show, Don't Tell (And Really Getting It) looks at one of the most frustrating aspects of writing—showing, and not telling. Learn what *show, don't tell* means, how to spot told prose in your writing, and when telling is the *right* thing to do. The book also explores aspects of writing that aren't technically telling, but are connected to told prose and can make prose feel told, such as infodumps, description, and backstory.

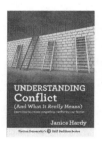

Understanding Conflict (And What It Really Means) looks at how to develop and create conflict in your fiction, and discusses the misconceptions about conflict that confuse and frustrate so many writers. The book also helps you understand what conflict really is, discusses the various aspects of conflict, and reveals why common advice on creating conflict doesn't always work.

Plotting Your Novel: Ideas and Structure shows you how to find and develop stories from that first spark of inspiration to the complete novel. It walks you through how to develop the right characters, find your setting, create your plot, as well as teach you how to identify where your novel fits in the market, and if your idea has what it takes to be a series. Ten self-guided workshops help you craft a solid plot. Each workshop builds upon the other to flesh out your idea as much or as little as you need to start writing, and contains guidance for plotters, pantsers, and everyone in between.

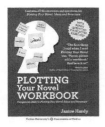

Plotting Your Novel Workbook is the companion guide to *Plotting Your Novel: Ideas and Structure* for those who like a hardcopy approach with easy-to-use worksheets. Its larger workbook format is perfect for writers who enjoy brainstorming on paper and developing their novels in an organized and guided format. No more searching for ideas jotted down on bits of paper. No more losing notes just when you need them most. With more than 100 exercises for the novel-planning process, you can keep all your thoughts in one handy place.

Fixing Your Character & Point-of-View Problems takes you step-by-step through revising character and character-related issues, such as two-dimensional characters, inconsistent points of view, excessive backstory, stale dialogue, didactic internalization, and lack of voice. She'll show you how to analyze your draft, spot any problems or weak areas, and fix those problems. Five self-guided workshops show you how to craft compelling characters, solid points of view, and strong character voices readers will love.

Fixing Your Plot & Story Structure Problems guides you through plot and story structure-related issues, such as wandering plots; a lack of scene structure; no goals, conflicts, or stakes; low tension; no hooks; and slow pacing. She'll show you how to analyze your draft, spot any problems or weak areas, and fix those problems. Five self-guided workshops show you how to craft gripping plots and novels that are impossible to put down.

Fixing Your Setting & Description Problems focuses on setting and description-related issues, such as weak world building, heavy infodumping, told prose, awkward stage direction, inconsistent tone and mood, and overwritten descriptions. She'll show you how to analyze your draft, spot any problems or weak areas, and fix those problems. Five self-guided workshops show you how to craft immersive settings and worlds that draw readers into your story and keep them there.

Acknowledgments

As always, this book would not be here without the help and support of some amazing people.

Serious thanks to my husband Tom. You put up with me every day and I can't thank you enough for that. Being married to a writer on a deadline is not easy, and you're always there with hot tea and treats when I need it.

To the best little crit partner ever—Ann Meier. I'm running out of ways to tell you, "thank you" so I'm going to just start sending chocolate. You're as good a friend as you are a critiquer. Probably better since you read all my rough early drafts, and no one deserves that much punishment.

Huge hugs to my beta readers on this book: Dario Ciriello, Cheryl Mansfield, and Claudia Pearson. Extra hugs for reading this in the tight timeframe I needed you to.

Thank you to my Fiction University readers. You guys are why I do this, and every time I get an email or comment from you saying how something I wrote helped you write, it totally makes my day.

Thank you all.

About the Author

Janice Hardy is the founder of Fiction University, a site dedicated to helping writers improve their craft. She writes both fiction and nonfiction.

Her nonfiction books include the Skill Builders series: *Understanding Show, Don't Tell (And Really Getting It)* and *Understanding Conflict (And What It Really Means)*, and the Foundations of Fiction series: *Plotting Your Novel: Ideas and Structure*, a self-guided workshop for planning or revising a novel; its companion guide, *Plotting Your Novel Workbook*; and the *Revising Your Novel: First Draft to Finished Draft* series.

She's also the author of the teen fantasy trilogy The Healing Wars, including *The Shifter*, *Blue Fire*, and *Darkfall*, from Balzer+Bray/Harper Collins. *The Shifter* was chosen by the Georgia Center for the Book for its 2014 list of "Ten Books All Young Georgians Should Read." It was also shortlisted for the Waterstones Children's Book Prize (2011) and The Truman Award (2011).

Janice lives in Central Florida with her husband, one yard zombie, two cats, and a very nervous freshwater eel.

Visit her author's site at janicehardy.com for more information, or visit fiction-university.com to learn more about writing.

Follow her at @Janice_Hardy for writing links.

Made in the USA
Las Vegas, NV
11 January 2024

84239933R00077